How to Dispose
of Your Stuff

Heavenly Uses for Earthly Goods

by
Bette Filley

Dunamis House

P.O. Box 321

Issaquah, WA 98027

Telephone: (425) 255-5274

Fax: (425) 277-8780

Copyright 2003

First Edition: December 2003

By Dunamis House

ISBN: 1-880405-10-5

Library of Congress Control Number: 2002090640

Filley, Bette E.

Foreword

If ever there was a book that needs to be written, it is this one, and I believe the Lord has had me in training for nearly 70 years to be the one to write it.

I was raised by an aunt, a single lady of very modest means who believed the Eleventh Commandment was "Thou Shalt Not Waste." Her life was a living testimony to the old saying that "little is much when God is in it." We were as poor as church mice, but we never did without.

In spite of having only an eighth grade education, she took in and raised a discarded child (me) without one penny of help from my natural parents. The most she ever earned was forty cents an hour, but in spite of that, she was the one the whole family and the community turned to when they needed help. The woman was a world-class expert in making something out of nothing. She was a living example of how blessed it is to give, even when you're in need yourself.

It wasn't until years later in the 1970's, while watching the 700 Club, that I heard about World Concern's program of collecting excess medicines and medical supplies from doctors' and dentists' offices to supply medical missionaries overseas. This was a ministry that would have been after Nanny's own heart. I signed up that very day, and for the next 26 years collected tons of life-saving medicines that would have otherwise gone to waste. I knew that for many of the ultimate recipients of those medicines, they might be the only medications they would ever have in their entire lives. World Concern treated every pill like gold.

Over those years, I was frequently asked if I could find a home for other unneeded items, and invariably some person or organization with exactly that need would come along within a day or two. It was exciting to watch God match need with supply.

Also as years went by, I saw the problems others had with excess "stuff." When a young lady I knew got married, she and her husband had two households of goods to combine. Then shortly, her new husband's parents both died, leaving an immense house packed full of their lifetime accumulation, large storage units full of the remains of a medical practice, and a substantial estate.

In spite of the fact that there was a very explicit will, the doctor's other sibling contested the will, and the parent's entire estate ended up in the pockets of avaricious lawyers. It was like watching a poorly written soap opera to see the parent's wishes for disposal of their effects contorted, misconstrued and fought over by lawyers at $250 an hour. The lesson it gave to me, a distant observer, was: do your own disposing. "Do your giving while you're living, then you're knowing where it's going."

More recently, another Christian lady I knew, a very spry and lucid senior, gave her sister Power of Attorney "just in case." One day, the lady had a bad fall that resulted in several broken teeth and a badly broken thumb. They were traumatic and uncomfortable injuries, but not life-threatening. But because of her age and the need for surgery on the thumb, she required a brief stay in the hospital. Then sadly instead of going home, her sister had her signed, sealed and delivered to a nursing home, permanently!

While she was still physically incapacitated, arrangements for selling her home were made, and her entire household of belongings was given to a salvage dealer in exchange for the job of emptying out her house. The lady had impeccable tastes and a fine collection of nice things. That dealer no doubt couldn't believe his good fortune to "inherit" her entire estate without even knowing her. This is what can happen when you sign a Power of Attorney. This dear lady thought she had plenty of time to dispose of her belongings, but her one fall changed it all.

If you have ever wondered why estate lawyers are so wealthy, wonder no more. All too often they too become the silent heir who eventually gets the whole estate. Their fees alone can consume vast fortunes.

I cite these examples to point out two things. The Christian doctor and his wife thought they had their affairs in order, with both children getting nice equal inheritances, and the remainder going to ministries they loved. In the second instance, the dear lady would likewise have wanted many of her belongings to go into the Lord's work had she been consulted. In both instances, the desires of these good people were thwarted, and a not a penny went to the Lord.

If you wish to avoid the kind of situations I have outlined, I pray that this book will inspire you to start today to dispose of your excess, and that you will be led to give into the hands of those who are praying at this very moment for what it is you have to give.

Bette Filley

A Word about Climbing Mountains of Stuff

That mountain of a job is before us. We all know we have to tackle it, but it's probably the most overwhelming task we've ever faced. Even thinking of doing it is tiring. Our challenge is named Mount Accumulation.

It's also traumatic. The task is so big, and we're so small. We don't know what route to follow, or how long it will take. Parts of our mountain are out of sight. They're in closets, basements, spare rooms, under beds, filling garages, barns crawl spaces, attics, junk drawers, second homes, work places, outbuildings, and storage units. Even if we ignore this mountain of a task, it won't go away. Someday, somebody will have to tackle it. Maybe we've collected so much stuff, it's not just one mountain, it's a whole range. The longer you look at it and worry about it, the bigger it looks.

When my husband and I moved to Washington State, we fell in love with its gorgeous mountains and took up mountaineering, and eventually became climbing instructors. My personal favorite peak is Mount Rainier, a beautiful 14,411' foot volcano about which I've written two books. It is one tough mountain that takes a long time to climb or even hike around. Dozens have died in the attempt to climb it. Yet even as daunting as it is, a paraplegic, several blind climbers, a twelve year old, and an 81 year old have conquered it. The same will be true of this peak we are facing. It *CAN* be reduced to molehill status, regardless of our age or physical capabilities.

Now let me share a little secret about climbing a mountain.

Over the years, I've gotten to know several world-class climbers, some who have even climbed Mount Everest. The secret is, that no matter how big and strong, experienced or famous the climbers may be, all mountains are climbed in exactly the same way, — one step at a time. Actually it's usually hundreds of small slow steps, with lots of stops to catch your breath between steps. So it will be as we climb Mount Accumulation. But I'm happy we report we don't have to climb it alone.

Remember that "Footprints in the Sand" story that went around a few years ago? Well the good news is that the Lord doesn't just walk on beaches. He climbs mountains too, and in fact is a very good guide. I suggest you don't just bring Him along, but put him in charge of this endeavor.

Making this a partnership will be the factor that will determine whether this adventure will be the hardest thing you've ever done, or one of the most rewarding and satisfying experiences of your life.

One thing that always must be decided on any big expedition, is who is going to carry the load. That's usually decided by "whose stuff is it?"

If ownership and possession is of utmost importance to you, you're going to carry it, and have a hard time parting with anything.

If you dedicate the load to the service of the Lord, He'll gladly carry it, and know exactly what to do with it. In fact, He's got many willing hands ready and able to come help and gladly take it off your hands.

With each step, each box, Mount Accumulation will diminish, and the Mountain of Blessings will grow across the valley.

Good planning and preparation is the key to success of any expedition, and this book is no exception. Many dear folks came along to help in compiling this "guidebook," and I am grateful to all of them. They are Mary Gilmore, Tom Velnosky, Frank Heuston, Jan DeVito, Gina Brueske, Julia Brueggeman, Jan Pancratz, Mary Schurman, Phyllis and Dick Filley, Tom Filley, Patricia Messenger, Barbara Sentino, Helen and George Evans, Patti Olson, Dennis and Doris Garrett, Mike, Susan, Mark, Rachel, Matthew and Harmony French, Marc Hill and John O'Day.

Thanks also to my dear husband Larry and daughter Kathy for allowing me to spend so many hundreds of hours on the computer.

So now it's time to get started, and it all begins with a single step.

Let's do it!

Bette Filley

Dedicated

To my dear cousin Margaret

Who never had the opportunity

To dispose of her own stuff

Legal Notice

Table of Contents

Chapter Fourteen
Medicines and Medical Aids

Chapter Fifteen
PAPERS, PAPERS, PAPERS

Chapter Sixteen
HOUSEHOLD GOODS

Chapter Seventeen
KITCHEN EQUIPMENT

Chapter Eighteen
COLLECTIONS

Chapter Nineteen
HOBBIES

Chapter Twenty
SPORTING GOODS

Chapter Twenty-Six
LIFE GIVING DONATIONS

Chapter Twenty-Seven
The Ultimate Arrangements

Chapter Twenty-Eight
MISCELLANEOUS

Chapter Twenty-Nine
HOW TO PREVENT REACCUMULATING

Chapter Thirty
RECIPIENT GROUPS AND WHAT THEY NEED

Chapter One

OUR BELONGINGS

The Howard Hughes Estate

Billy Graham was holding a Crusade in Seattle when multi-millionaire Howard Hughes died. That evening Billy left his audience with a colossal teaser: "Come tomorrow night, and I'll tell you how much Howard Hughes left."

The next night the Kingdome was packed. The newspapers were full of speculative articles about how much Hughes was worth. Billy implied that he had inside knowledge. As soon as the song service was over, he gave the crowd the answer as promised.

"Howard Hughes left it *all!*"

The moral of that story is that we, too, will some-day leave it all.

The purpose of this book is to provide a resource for when, where, and how to dispose of that "all," whatever our "all" is.

Materialism: The All-American Way

Each generation, it seems, is more materialistic than the one that preceded it. We're constantly bombarded with cute slogans encouraging us to acquire more: "Shop Till You Drop." "Buy Till you Die." "Spend To The End."

We earn, buy, make, accumulate, acquire, bank, cache, collect, amass, gather, get, glean, garner, inherit, keep, maintain, nest-egg, obtain, preserve, procure, save, squirrel, stack, stash, stockpile, store up, stow, and hoard as if there were no tomorrow. We're a nation of pack rats. No wonder the storage unit business is booming!

Where will it all end? It will end when we either personally make the decisions about what to do with it all, or when someone has to make those decisions for us.

For we brought nothing into the world, and we can take nothing out of it.

(I Tim. 6:7 NIV)

Deciding to Decide

For some, the resolve to reverse the accumulation process comes when they realize they aren't free to retire and enjoy life. One day they come to the realization that it's not they who own their possessions, but their possessions that own them. They've become locked into a life of caring, feeding, cleaning, maintaining, mowing and repairing.

Many a retiree has discovered that less is more. Less stuff to clean and maintain equals more time for other interests. Time and freedom, they discover, are commodities as valuable as a house full of belongings.

Some seek to use their retirement years to become snowbirds and spend their winter months in a better climate, or to travel, take up new interests and attempt to make the most of, and enjoy, what's left of life. This option frequently begins with major material downsizing. Some take the leap to move out the family homestead and into a condo or town house, hit the road in a motor home or 5th wheeler, sail the world in a yacht or sailboat, or to move to Florida or Arizona. Not all are capable of accomplishing this purpose, but many of the suntanned set that have taken up the gypsy life have done so and love it. The only hill they're over is the hill of amassed "stuff."

Once the kids are grown and gone, a big house with an accumulation of belongings is a *huge* responsibility. A man may retire from his job, but a woman can never retire from hers if she lives in a house full of possessions either she can't bear to part with, or isn't allowed to dispose of.

.a man's life does not consist in the abundance of his possessions

Luke 12:15

The answer, if wanting to stay in the family home, is to simplify: move into or utilize a smaller portion of it, or share it with children and their families (think twice and then thrice about this option) or with friends. That's one way to stay in "this old house" with someone else doing the maintenance. Still others go to live with their children in *their* homes. All these options have one thing in common. All require getting rid of a great deal of "stuff."

Still others decide to enjoy retirement by selling their homes and moving to one of the many nice active adult communities, retirement homes, assisted living centers, or active senior living arrangements and lifestyles. The common denominator they usually share is that someone else handles all the responsibilities of building maintenance, lawn care and, frequently, even cooking and cleaning. These moves, too, generally require disposing of part or all of entire households of goods and personal effects.

Then there are those who marry, or remarry, late in life and must combine two households, or those who decide to sail off into the sunset in style, on a live-aboard yacht or sailboat. For every "down-sizing" for an unhappy reason, there are dozens of joyous ones! A surprising number of retired seniors take up second careers as missionaries and sell their homes to finance their ministry.

For many, it isn't a matter of *wanting* to downsize, it's a matter of financial survival. They're being eaten alive by ever-escalating property taxes, gargantuan utility bills, astronomical medical bills, and skyrocketing insurance premiums. These all hit about the same time the house starts showing its age and needing many expensive repairs, upkeep and remodeling. Many sadly find that owning their home free and clear doesn't bring the financial relief they thought it would. The appreciated real estate values also mean inflated taxes and the tax bills alone can amount to more than they used to spend on just mortgage payments.

The sad fact is, these days, many seniors just get taxed out of their homes.

Another reason many seniors "down-size" is control. They want to be the ones who decide what becomes of their belongings, rather than have it decided for them. They believe it's better to make lifestyle changes when they want to and are able to, rather than wait until they must. They go into the process with a positive attitude, focusing on the benefits the change will bring. Seeing their goods fully used, en-

But store up for yourselves treasures in heaven, where moth and rust do not destroy, and where thieves do not break in and steal. For where your treasure is, there your heart will be also

Matthew 6:19-21

joyed and appreciated by the new recipients of their choice gives them a tremendous sense of satisfaction, rather one of loss.

And finally, remember the old story about the fellow who asked three people when life begins?

The first answered, "at conception."

The second answered, "at birth."

The third answered, "when the dog dies and the kids leave home."

To which many retirees would add, "and when we sell the house and we leave too."

The bottom line? Good-bye "stuff."

Young People Accumulate, Too

Seniors aren't the only ones who may be forced to dispose of a house full of goods. It happens to younger people too, through:

- o Divorce
- o Marriage and the need to consolidate two households
- o Inheritance of a house full of someone else's goods
- o The sudden loss of a loved one
- o The unexpected loss of a job
- o Moving "back home" with parents
- o Moving overseas
- o Caretaker responsibilities finished
- o The decision to travel extensively
- o The desire to live more simply
- o The necessity to reduce clutter
- o The need to get out of debt
- o Going into the military
- o Getting a new job across country, and no money to move.
- o Owning rental property and having a renter vacate, leaving all their belongings.

Giving to God reminds us who He is, who we are, and what our relationship should be to the things He has allowed us to manage in His name.

Larry Burkett

founder, Christian Financial Concepts

o The arrival of a baby, which frequently requires "making room" by getting rid of the
Chippendale lest it become chipped-all-
over.

Moving companies base charges on weight and
bulk, and it's frequently cheaper to sell heavy household goods rather than to move them. Belongings
can always be replaced at the other end through
shrewd shopping involving the used furniture and
appliance ads, auctions, garage sales and thrift
stores.

**It is more blessed
to give than to
receive**

Acts 20:35

Choosing Not To Choose

Of course there are many people who don't dispose of their possessions, or who postpone the decision too long. It's hard to make the arrangements
from a nursing home, and more difficult still to make
them from the great beyond. This book is for both
those who handle the job themselves or those who
must do the job for others.

How to Dispose of your Stuff

Chapter Two

GODLY GIVING

The Manufacturer's Handbook

The reason so many people die without wills is because drawing one up requires finally facing the dreaded job of facing up to "settling one's affairs" and the accompanying thoughts of what the future holds. It also usually forces confronting their lifelong postponement of the haunting questions of mortality, the reality of God, Eternity, Heaven and Hell. Such people may tend to hunker down with a "Heck no, I won't go" mentality, as if hanging onto their world possessions is going to stop them from going.

The Bible admonishes us to have compassion for the poor and disabled, but not the lazy.

The answer lies in the old cliché, "when all else fails, read the directions." The only instructions human beings came with are "the Manufacturer's Handbook," — the Bible. For the benefit of those who may not realize that the Bible has quite a bit to say about our earthly belongings, as well as the disposal of them, we include this brief study of the subject.

Remember that old fable about a child being born with a silver spoon in its mouth? Well some babies may have been born with one, but the Bible does say the spoon will stay here when they leave. "Naked we came into this world, and naked we shall return." Penniless! No U-Haul truck with all our worldly belongings will follow us to the great hereafter.

But there's another old cliché, the one that says "you can't take it with you." That's true, but did you know, *you can ship it on ahead!!*

Call the Eternal Treasure Shipping Company

No, you won't find the address in the Yellow Pages, you'll find it in the white pages of the Bible, in Matthew 19: 21.

Jesus told a rich young ruler, "If thou wilt be perfect, go and sell that thou hast, and give to the poor, and thou shall have treasure in heaven: and come and follow me." This story is repeated four more times in Mark 10:21 and Luke 18:22 and confirmed again in I Timothy 6:19 and Acts 10:4.

So here Jesus tells us how we are to accomplish this little miracle. With every item we put into the Lord's service, we're laying up treasure in heaven. We've all heard the expression, "one man's trash is another man's treasure," but the truth is, when you put an item into use in the Lord's service, it becomes treasure for both recipient and giver! " It is "recycled" to someone who can be blessed by it here on earth, and simultaneously "shipped on ahead" and credited to your heavenly account.

Who are the poor as defined by the Bible?

The poor **worked**

Deuteronomy
24:14 NIV

There are at least 204 references to the poor in the Bible. They include widows, orphans, the fatherless, the needy, the oppressed, the brokenhearted, the sick, the blind, invalids, the halt (cripples), the lame, those deaf and mute, those paralyzed (John 5:3), those withered, the elderly (John 21:18), those who have suffered disaster, the homeless, those without friends, the abandoned, the lepers, the disfigured, the naked, the dying, broken men and aliens.

Christ said, "inasmuch as ye have done it unto one of the least of these my brethren, ye have done it unto me." (Matthew 25:40).

"The least of these" also referred to the helpless, invalids, those incapable of taking care of themselves, the child-like, the retarded, and the mentally impaired.

How do we know what to give? Again, we can look the examples Jesus himself gave. "I was naked and you clothed me, hungry and you fed me, thirsty and you gave me to drink." Note He said *give them the things they need!* Food, clothing, water, and basic necessities of life. Notice too, it was very personal, one-on-one.

What about those on Welfare?

In biblical times, there were no welfare or "entitlement" programs or government mandated "wealth redistribution" schemes. Nobody was entitled to anything from the government, and idleness was not rewarded. "Poor" did not mean slackards or those partaking of government largess.

Many Americans make the mistake of thinking of today's welfare class as the poor, but the poor in America are rich when using world standards of comparison. Someone on the bottom tenth of U.S. income would still rank above 2/3 of world income standards.

Government welfare has distorted our whole concept of "cheerful giving", since our contributions (taxes) are not given voluntarily, and many of the recipients are "poor" by choice, not by chance. The poor who were physically-able in biblical times *worked* for their food. They gleaned it from the fields and vineyards after the reapers and pickers were finished working them.

Today the government has made itself the great benefactor, through the forced extraction of exorbitant taxes from Working Peter, to support Welfare Paul. To make matters worse, Peter's wife frequently has to go work too, so Paul's wife can lounge at home anticipating the check that will come in the first of the month. Most of the poor referred to in this book are not those who look to the government to provide their way of life, we refer here to the deserving poor as defined by the Bible.

The key to whether people deserve help comes from the biblical injunction which directs, "Those who **will not work**, neither should they eat." For instance, we have hundreds of thousands of loggers, miners, mill workers, ranchers, farmers and just ordinary people who have had their means of livelihood extinguished by their own government. They have been driven into bankruptcy (and in many cases, onto welfare) through no fault of their own.

> Each of us must have a desire to work if we are to accomplish what God put us on this earth to do. When someone wants assistance, a Christian should ask, "Is he asking me to supply his needs, wants, or desires? Does this individual really have an internal commitment to work?" It is possible to hinder God's perfect plan in another's life by satisfying his or her requests
>
> **Larry Burkett**
>
> **founder, Christian Financial Concepts**

These salt-of-the-earth people would love to work, but their jobs have been sacrificed at the altar of political correctness. Under today's topsy-turvy agenda, rats, weeds, salamanders, bugs, owls and fish are more important than human beings and their employment.

Frequently if these disenfranchised folks do find work, they become the working poor. Once the economic base (logging, mining or whatever) has been ripped out from under a community, the few jobs left usually do not pay enough to support a family, let alone pay for things like health insurance and sending children to college. What a cruel sentence to impose on good people who only wanted to work hard and play by the rules.

These politically dispossessed folks don't want welfare, they want to work and deserve all the help they can get!

What's Wrong With Government Spending To Help The Needy?

Let's see what Horatio Bunce had to say:

But if any provide not for his own, and specially for those of his own house, he hath denied the faith, and is worse than an infidel. (I Tim. 5:8)

"In the first place, the government ought to have in the Treasury no more than enough for its legitimate purposes. The power of collecting and disbursing money at pleasure is the most dangerous power that can be entrusted to man, particularly under our system of collecting revenue by a tariff, which reaches every man in the country, no matter how poor he may be, and the poorer he is, the more he pays in proportion to his means.

"While you are contributing to relieve one, you are drawing it from thousands who are even worse off than he. If you have the right to give anything, the amount is simply a matter of discretion with you, and you had as much right to give $20,000,000 as $20,000.

"If you have the right to give to one, you have the right to give to all; and, as the Constitution neither defines charity nor stipulates the amount, you are at liberty to give to any and everything which you *believe,* or *profess to believe,* is a charity, and to any amount you think proper.

"You will very easily perceive what a wide door this would open for fraud and corruption and favoritism, on the one hand, and for robbing the people on the other.

"No, Colonel, Congress has no right to give charity. Individual members may give as much of their own money as they please, but they have no right to touch a dollar of the public money for that purpose.

"The people have delegated to Congress, by the Constitution, the power to do certain things. To do these, it is authorized to collect and pay moneys, and for nothing else. Everything beyond this is usurpation, and a violation of the Constitution."

- Horatio Bunce, to Colonel Davy Crockett, about a vote in Congress to give $20,000 to victims of a large fire.

(From the National Center for Constitutional Studies)

Do not withhold good from those who *deserve* it, when it is in your power to act.

What the Bible says about Giving

The Bible has many admonitions about giving. Numbers 7 alone devotes all of its 89 verses, almost 2,000 words, to giving. The Torah (the first five books of the Old Testament) likewise contains a variety of laws applying to the poor.

Deuteronomy 15:7-11 tells us "the poor will always be among you." So what has historically been done with the poor before the government got into the charity business? Human nature hasn't changed since biblical times. That means there have always

Don't wait for extraordinary opportunities. Seize common occasions and make them great.
-Orison Swett Marden-

been people who were incapable of caring for themselves, and generous people who have always seen to their needs.

The first unit of governance in the bible is the family, under the headship of the father. Thus it was (and still is) the family's responsibility to care for their own. "But if any provide not for his own, and especially for those of his own house, he hath denied the faith, and is worse than an infidel." 1 Timothy 5:8 has never been revised.

The second tier of responsibility, for those who had no families (widows and orphans), fell on the church. We read in the New Testament that the early church took those responsibilities seriously. Many churches still do, and have a continuing need for the basic necessities of food, clothing, jobs and housing which they use to help the poor.

Until the inception of welfare, family homes usually contained several generations. The old were not put out to fend for themselves when they could no longer work, and young people were expected to pitch in and contribute to the general welfare of the family at very early ages. Even after a young couple married, the common practice was to either build an addition onto the house, or build another home on the family property. Acquisitions belonged communally to the family, and we talk about many of these types of family possessions as "heirlooms" in this book.

Luxuries were much more sparse in "the good old days." And people lived by the admonition that "a man's life does not consist in the abundance of his possessions" as told in Luke 12:15. In fact, among a man's greatest treasures were his good name and his word, not his material belongings. This was based on Proverbs 11:1, which states, "a good name is rather to be chosen than great riches, and loving favor rather than silver and gold."

In less than a century, families have abdicated their responsibilities and now the members of each generation go their own way, feeling little obligation to be concerned about the needs of their relatives. Wily politicians ever seeking reelection have encouraged this mentality by promising that Uncle Sam will take care of everyone from cradle to grave.

Today it isn't uncommon to read of obscenely wealthy people whose parents are living in poverty. Even millionaire congressmen tell us tales of their parents who can't afford medications, as if we are supposed to feel sorry for them. They see themselves as successful, but Christian charity is nowhere to be found in them.

The lesson for us today in disposing of our goods, is to first address the needs within our own family. This not selfish, it is scriptural. When those needs are met, then look to the needs of those around you.

More about Leaving to One's Own

In addition to giving to the poor, there's one other group we are admonished to give to, this time in the form of an inheritance.

"A good man leaves an inheritance for his children's children." Proverbs 13:22 – NIV)

The key question, is what exactly is an inheritance?

The legal definition, according to Blackstone, is "a perpetual or continuing right to which a man and his heirs have to an estate; an estate which a man has by descent as heir to another, or which he may transmit to another as his heir; an estate derived from an ancestor to an heir in course of law."

The word "inheritance" (used simply) is mostly confined to the title of land and tenements by a descent." – Mozley

"Men are not proprietors of what they have, merely for themselves; their children have a title to part of it which comes to be wholly theirs when death has put an end to their parents' use of it; and this we call inheritance." – Locke

Simply put, it is belongings of worth, property and valuable possessions.

> I shall pass through this world but once. Any good therefore that I can do, or any kindness that I can show to any human being, let me do it now. Let me not defer nor neglect it, for I shall not pass this way again.
>
> -Stephen Grellet-

The scriptural admonition is restated from a different perspective in 2 Corinthians 12:4. "After all, children should not save up for their parents, but parents for their children."

In other words, leaving our children and grandchildren an inheritance is not an option. God says, "do it!"

Other Biblical References about Giving

Proverbs 19:17 tells us that "giving to the poor is lending to the Lord," and in Luke 6:38 we're admonished "Give, and it shall be given unto you; good measure, pressed down, and shaken together, and running over, shall men give into your bosom. For with the same measure that ye mete withal it shall be measured to you again."

Actually with that scripture, God laid down the principal of giving, followed by both earthly and heavenly reward. Those 40 simple words contain the keys to both a fulfilled life here on earth, and the promise of treasure laid up in heaven.

So when you give, God gives back more. If you give furniture, that doesn't mean He's going to load you up with more furniture. He is the giver of all good gifts beyond your wildest dreams In addition to granting the desires of your heart, God's gifts are things like health, restored relationships, jobs and children.

One of our "assignments" as Christians (God's present day disciples) is to let God's love show through us. We are to do as He would do. When we give earthly goods to the (truly) poor, we are doing what Jesus would do. He wouldn't have given a Skid Road drunk money to buy more alcohol, He would have given him a good meal, and probably his cloak and blanket too.

Let God use you. Count your blessings. At this very moment, people are praying for those very items that you no longer need.

14

Chapter Three

EARTHLY GIVING

This Stuff Shall Rise Again

There is an excellent reason to give material goods to worthy organizations. If you give them the *things* they can use for those they help, then that's less money they will require to purchase those same items (usually at retail) and that much more they'll have to spend on other needs.

As America enters into welfare reform and the federal government turns over $55 billion of welfare funding back to the states, it is expecting much of the monetary burden to be picked up by philanthropic and non-profit fund raising organizations. Thus, the demands on such organizations will skyrocket.

In the 1990's, federal and state funding for non-profit charities dropped 37 percent. Congress is counting (unrealistically) on private giving to increase 60 percent to make up for the shortfall caused by the government cuts. The fact is that public giving increases 1 percent to 3 percent a year after inflation. Thus charities, already scrambling to make ends meet, are going to have to find new ways to make their resources go farther, and will become more dependent upon voluntary gifts and services. Your little gift of no-longer needed items may seem like a tiny drop in the bucket, but a bucket of water is merely an accumulation of many little drops.

Charitable Tax Deductions

Our government also recognizes the value of "goods", which is why they give tax deductions for non-cash contributions to charitable organizations. Such qualified organizations include churches, synagogues and other religious institutions, most nonprofit educational organizations, public parks and recreational facilities, physical affliction groups and a multitude of charitable special interest groups.

> "When we do the best we can, we never know what miracle is wrought in our life, or in the life of another."
> ~Helen Keller~

As government embarks on the massive re-vamping of the nation's welfare system, and expects people to donate more to offset the costs of helping the poor at the local level, many hope that congress will proportionately increase the size of the charitable tax deduction. But don't count your increased deduction blessings yet. One camp argues that the government should not be in the business of promoting individual giving habits, while at the other extreme, some believe donors should receive a tax *credit* for charitable contributions. God loves a cheerful giver, but it remains to be seen how cheerful Uncle Sam will be over the giver's giving.

However, whether you get a tax deduction or not, do your giving for the right reason. Do it because it is good stewardship, and puts to good use that which you no longer need.

That Good Samaritan we know from Luke 10:33 came upon a wounded man who had been beaten by robbers, and met that man's immediate physical needs. He washed his wounds and bound them up, then put the man on his own donkey and took him to an inn. There he saw to it that the man was cared for and nursed back to health. He not only left money to pay for the man's care, but also gave the promise that if it cost more, he would pay that too upon his return. And he did all this out of the goodness of his heart, because he had compassion for his fellow man. He did all this without the knowledge that he was laying up treasure in heaven, and with no thought of repayment or a tax write-off.

> "Give me five minutes with a person's checkbook, and I will tell you where their heart is." — Billy Graham (1918-)

Compare him to the stingy man who begrudgingly put a quarter in the offering plate. He later discovered he had mistakenly given a Susan B. Anthony silver dollar instead. Distraught, he anguished to his friend how upset he was over giving more than the quarter. "Don't worry," said his friend. "Since that was your intention, God will only give you credit for the quarter."

God really does know your heart, and your intentions.

Don't give because of the tax deduction, or because you'll be rewarded in heaven. Don't give for the thanks or earthly adulation. Give because it's more blessed to give than to receive. Give because you'll be helping someone who really needs help, and by doing so, you'll be pleasing God. He who knows the number of hairs on your head, and every sparrow that falls to the earth, also knows your heart, your deeds and your intentions.

Charity of the heart doesn't care if it's tax deductible or not.

Why Others Give

A recent survey conducted by the Independent Sector, a Washington, D.C.-based coalition of charities, found that the main motivating factor among those who donate either money, goods, or time and service to charities, was not to get a tax deduction.

The study, entitled "Giving and Volunteering," determined that 88 percent said they gave because of personal door-to-door solicitation; 87 percent because of their own past volunteer work experience; 85 percent because they frequent religious services; 81 percent because a friend asked; 80 percent because others helped them; 79 percent in order to make a significant social change; and 63 percent because a clergy member asked.

Whatever their reasons, in 1993, 32 million itemizers gave about $63 billion to charity.

Guidelines for Christian Giving

If your goal is to put your donated goods into the Lord's service, pray for guidance and wisdom as to what to do with each item and to whom to give.

Realize that you are simply the vessel the Lord is using to get items into the next hands where the things are needed. Give the items to the Lord and look upon the organizations doing the receiving as simply channels the Lord is using too.

When you give with open hands and a pure heart, God knows your intentions. When you give unto the Lord, what happens to your gift after you give it is not between you and the organization, but is then

What we give to institutions is soon forgotten, what we give to indivituals is always remembered.
-Uknown-

between the organization and God. (If they misuse the contribution, then they will be accountable to God).

Recognize that once you give your belongings to the Lord, they're then His, and you can sit back and watch Him dispose of them. Just be receptive to that still small voice that will bring people and groups (that you probably never knew existed) to your attention. Being a part of the "Heavenly Disposal Company" may be the most exhilarating and rewarding thing you've ever done. It's pretty exciting to be in partnership with God.

Expect miracles. You will see a lot of them when you start giving goods at the Lord's direction.

Common Sense Rules for Donating

1. Never, EVER be pressured into giving anything! Look on pressure as a red flag! Don't let anyone use your kindness and generosity to take advantage of you. Take a step back and reevaluate. The charity that needs money *TODAY* will still need it tomorrow. Watch out for pitches that are long on emotion, and short on facts.

2. NEVER give cash without first doing some investigating. If for some reason you do give money, write out a check. Look at the name carefully. Some dishonest charities have names that sound the same as legitimate ones. Be sure you're giving to the organization that you really intend to give to.

3. Don't hesitate to ask the charity to provide detailed *written* information about its programs and finances before you give. Charities with nothing to hide will welcome your interest.

4. When perusing financial statements, look for the percentage of funds spent on administrative overhead versus the amount used to directly help the needy or intended recipients.

IRS Rules For Deductions

1. Individuals giving time or services get no deduction except for out-of-pocket expenses and mileage.

2. Cash contributions require proof via a receipt. Under the recently revised tax law, canceled checks are no longer considered substantiation for each and every donation of $250 or more. A specific written receipt from the charitable organization is necessary.

3. For gifts of goods (called "in-kind" gifts) charities are required by law to give donors a receipt listing the items they donated. However it is up to the donor to estimate the value of the gift. The amount you can use as a charitable deduction is based on the fair market value of the property when you donate it. Fair market value is defined as "the price at which property would change hands between a willing buyer and a willing seller."

The real measure of our wealth is how much we'd be worth if we lost all our money.
-J.H. Jowett-

4. Report your contributions on Schedule A of your federal tax return. For gifts of property exceeding $500 per item or groups of similar items, request IRS form 8283, - "Non-cash Charitable Contributions". The donor must complete this form in order to claim a charitable contribution deduction on the donor's tax return. Request that the Donee (the group to whom the gift is given) sign the Donee Acknowledgement Section on behalf of the recipient.

5. When a gift is thought to exceed $5,000 in value, donors must provide a certified appraisal, and the cost of the appraisal is the responsibility of the donor.

(Note: these IRS rules are as of publication of this book. Consult your tax expert for questions about your deductions.)

Ben Franklin Theology

Dost thou love life?

Then do not squander time, for that's the stuff life is made of.

-Benjamin Franklin- (1706-1790), "Poor Richard's Almanac"

Many of old Ben's proverbs had to do with waste, such as "Waste not, want not." Ben was incredibly frugal and ingenious at utilizing every shred of everything. But Ben got his inspiration from the Bible.

Another of Ben Franklin's famous quips was "a woman can throw out more with a teaspoon than a man can bring in with a shovel." That one is based on Proverbs 14:1 that says, "Every wise woman buildeth her house, but the foolish plucketh it down with her hands." In other words, she's a waster.

Giving with Discernment

One of the best reasons for contributing *goods* to worthy organizations is that the full contribution is used. No solicitors or paid fund-raisers will skim off a portion of your contribution. More and more frequently, it's coming to light that as much as 95% of funds contributed via telephone solicitation, for instance, never make it to the intended charity, or to the needy recipients. In far too many cases, the money is siphoned off to fund-raising and administration costs, or as we've sadly seen in the aftermath of 9/11, just plain larceny and deception.

However whatever the contribution may be, don't be afraid to ask for written information about the designated charity. A group's annual report should have descriptions of the group's activities and a complete financial statement. Nonprofit organizations are required by law to make full disclosure of receipts and expenditures (including fund raising costs) by way of filing IRS Form 990, on an annual basis.

Your state attorney general or Secretary of State will also most likely have the information on non-profit organizations operating in within your state boundaries, or you can get it from the state where the group is headquartered. Also, your Better Business Bureau can often get information from its Philanthropic Advisory Service — the National Charities Information Bureau (19 Union Square West, New York, NY 10003).

The American Institute of Philanthropy (4579 Lac Lede Avenue, Suite 136, St. Louis, MO 63108) also offers information on specific charities.

For information about the Better Business Bureau's charity evaluations, call 703-276-0100. The reports are also available on the agency's Internet web site: http://www.bbb.org.

The Evangelical Council for Financial Accountability can provide information on Christian charities, ministries and nonprofit organizations. ECFA can be reached at:

Evangelical Council for Financial Accountability
P. O. Box 17456
Washington, DC 20041-0456
Telephone: 800-3BE-WISE (800-323-9473)
FAX: 540-535-0533
E-mail: info@ecfa.org
Website: http://webmaster@ecfa.org

Finally, if donating money, don't pay with cash or a credit card. Always pay by check and make the check out to the charity, using the full name of the group, not initials. Mail your check directly to the charity, not to the fundraiser.

> The true friend is never used or abused, but rather enjoyed through the joy of rendering service to him.

We are all bombarded daily with requests for donations from every imaginable type of organization. Competition for nonprofit dollars is fierce. Unfortunately, some groups are unscrupulous. Their telephone solicitations are particularly offensive. They use such unethical approaches as fabricated emergencies, fear, guilt, intimidation, and any number or ruses to get a contribution. They succeed in getting money on an average of one out of every 10 calls.

As donors, we must use our heads as well as our hearts when deciding where to give our time and dollars.

ECFA's Donor's Bill of Rights

If giving to a Christian organization, make sure they abide by the ECFA's (Evangelical Council for Financial Accountability's) "Donor's Bill of Rights."

You have the right to:

1. Know how the funds of an organization are being spent.
2. Know what the programs you support are accomplishing.
3. Know that the organization is in compliance with federal, state and municipal laws.
4. Restrict or designate your gifts to a particular project.
5. A response to your inquiries about finances and programs.
6. Visit offices and program sites of an organization to talk personally with the staff.
7. Not be high-pressured into giving to any organization.
8. Know that the organization is well managed.
9. Know that there is a responsible governing board and who these board members are.
10. Know that all appeals for funds are truthful and accurate.

A journey of a thousand miles begins with a single step.
   -Chinese Proverb

The Evangelical Council for Financial Accountability (ECFA) was founded in 1979. It is comprised of almost 1,000 charitable, religious, missionary, social and educational tax-exempt nonprofit 501 (c) (3) organizations.

Chapter Four

GETTING ORGANIZED

If disposing of someone else's estate

If you are the executor of someone else's estate, begin by making a very detailed written inventory. A relative with a sharp memory may challenge you if a certain item isn't accounted for, so for your own protection, keep very explicit records. If you can't account for missing items, you may be getting a call from a lawyer, the police or the IRS.

First, immediately do a quick walk-through to identify and gather the valuables: Gold, silver, gems, antiques, stocks, deeds, diaries, the will and other important papers, etc. Remove them from the premises and put them in a safe deposit box or other secure location. Unfortunately one class of particularly cruel thieves makes it a practice to study the obituaries and make midnight calls that are not for the intention of expressing their condolences. Thus it is important to *immediately* secure anything anyone may want to steal. Sadly it also isn't uncommon for unscrupulous relatives to prematurely "appropriate" what they think should be theirs.

You might even consider photographing or videotaping the contents of each room, and carrying a tape recorder, describing the contents as you go.

Remember to set aside a certain amount of money from the estate for postage and for shipping items because not all recipients may be local, and not all charities may be able to afford shipping.

If in doubt, or if there is the potential for controversy, ask for court supervision.

Rules for Disposing of Someone Else's Goods

If no instructions for disposition of anything were made, and you find yourself as legal executor with the job of cleaning out the house to settle the estate, approach your task with prayer, care and deliberation, and a *reputable* lawyer! Change the locks if you

> Give only that which is yours to give lest others take that which is your own

must, but don't allow relatives and treasure hunters to come in and help themselves to the booty. As stated above, *remove valuables to a secure location.*

Unfortunately the covetous thoughts of a obtaining the deceased's valuable belongings brings out the worst in many people, and history abounds with horror stories of larceny, lying, and deceit of every imaginable description by otherwise honorable people. All of this over what the Bible calls "wood, hay, and stubble," the term used for our earthly works and possessions. (I Corinthians 3:11-15).

Approach your task as a sacred trust with the Golden Rule as your guiding credo. Treat the deceased's belongings as you would have others treat yours. Don't hold an "open house" to show nosey people how someone lived or what they owned. Don't gossip or spread salacious stories over what you might find.

Don't let young children anywhere around "the estate" or belongings you are disposing of. Children have no idea of the value of what they might be touching, and dirty or sticky little hands can do irreparable damage to things which years later they might long to possess. If the deceased would not allow children to paw through their belongings, then you shouldn't either!

If Disposing of Your Own Goods

A financial counselor will jokingly tell you that the ideal amount of savings and investments a person should have are those which will give you enough to live comfortably, and then run out as the last penny is spent on the day you die. This creates a tricky timing challenge, to be sure. On the material side, it's a matter of quality of life.

As we get older and our retirement years appear on the horizon, most people look upon retirement as the time when they stop acquiring and start

How refreshing, the whinny of a packhorse unloaded of everything!

Old Chinese saying

disposing. The ideal goal should really be to have every last thing disposed of or assigned to its new home as our need for it expires.

Most people feel uncomfortable with the thought of someone else going through their belongings. Strangers will have no regard for the fond memories items evoke, and sentimental treasures might be looked upon as trash by some future beholder. Many are reluctant to have others put in a position to examine evidence of their innermost private lives. Privacy they so jealously guarded all their days will be invaded as others rummage through their personal possessions. The very thought can be abhorrent.

The beginning is the half of every action – Greek Proverb

This can all be avoided by doing the disposing yourself. As the old admonition says, "Do your giving while you're living. Then you're knowing where it's going."

Start planning NOW! Don't wait until an emergency forces rapid dispersal or disposal. Set small goals and begin now to dispose of no longer needed, wanted or used items.

Make a longhand detailed list of who is to get each item.

With things you are still using, tape labels to the bottom of the article designating the future recipient and add the item to your written list of instructions.

If one (charitable) group turns you down or isn't interested or able to take your contribution, don't give up. Ask them if they know of any others who might be, or go on to the next prospect on your list. Most similar charities and ministries usually know about others with the same mission and will be glad to refer you.

How to Dispose of your Stuff

Chapter Five

HOW TO START DISPOSING

The best place is to begin is at the grocery store, to pick up some sturdy cardboard boxes. (But be sure the boxes not so big that you can't lift them when they're full). Using a big black pen, mark each box as to end recipient, organization or destination, and line them up out of your traffic pattern, so that as you sort, you can begin to fill boxes.

Using the marked box method, you can take just two or three boxes into a room for an initial sort. For instance you might want to make up a box each for a men's mission, a domestic abuse shelter and an AIDS hospice. Starting in the bathroom, the mission box will get all the partial containers of shaving cream, athlete's foot spray, mouthwash (taking care that you don't include any which is alcohol-based, since they may drink it), soap, clean combs, razors and deodorant.

The box for the women's shelter could get soap, deodorant, perfume, powder, cosmetics, shampoo, conditioner, feminine products, and brushes.

The hospice box could contain soft towels and washcloths, skin lotions and throat lozenges. Bigger organizations will only take new unopened containers, but you'll find that many small local groups are happy to get even partial bottles of notions.

As the boxes get full, you can either drop them off, or call the charity to come pick them up. Don't be discouraged if it takes a while until you see a dent in the remaining goods.

Just remember, they call this stuff "goods" because it is good! If you were in desperate need of the item and were to receive it, it would indeed be *very* good. Thus as the disposer, your job is to find who it would be good for. The sooner you begin, the sooner the goods can be put back into service by their new owner.

> **"Whenever you set out to do something, something else must always be done first."**
> **Murphy's Law #12**

Finding Recipients

There are a number of ways to dispose of material goods, but this book attempts to suggest the most appropriate home for each item. We realize it would take a considerable amount of time to dispose of every single item in this manner, but if you aren't in any rush to do the job, you can do a great deal of good in the community.

You can always quit at any time, and just call Salvation Army, Goodwill or one of the many other organizations that run large thrift stores to come get the whole load. Even if you only have the time or energy to follow through on a few of these recommendations, that's better than none at all. Every single item put into the hands of someone who truly needs it is a victory.

Also, if you are thinking of retiring, moving or scaling down in a few years, you should begin disposing *now.* Start with the most dispensable items. You'll have plenty of time to sort and gather, and set small goals of so many items or boxes per week or month. Remember, if it took you 60 years to accumulate all these belongings, it's going to take a long time (ideally months or years) to dispose of several tons of stuff.

A man is not where he lives, but where he loves. -Latin Proverb-

There are also Good Samaritans out there who are natural "match-makers". They help people with needs find those who can fill that need. We knew of one woman who had a refrigerator ministry. She worked for landlords, as the person who cleaned out apartments between tenants, so she had a continual supply of refrigerators as they were being replaced by newer models.

The fridges barely had time to defrost before she found a grateful new owner. Other such "stuff match-makers" are frequently church secretaries and Senior Center secretaries or social workers. They continually get calls from people in need, so you might let several of them know that you have furniture, beds, mattresses, or whatever, available for donation.

Letting Recipients Find You

Another good way to find worthy recipients is to let them find you. As you get down to items that might be difficult to donate, run an ad such as the follows, and see who responds:

"FREE to those in need, or those who help others: men's shoes, size 10-1/2, fabric scraps, canning jars, garden tools, old gas range (works well), scrap iron, and Christmas decorations. Call 555-9211 between 4-6 p.m."

Some local papers will even run ads at no cost when the advertiser is offering items at no cost. If you don't want to be besieged with phone calls, use a Post Office box or have responses mailed to the newspaper (if they have that service). If you can avoid it, don't run the ad in a big metropolitan paper, since advertising in them can be very expensive. Instead try either a "Little Nickel" or whatever your area shopper is called, or small trade journal.

Perhaps you'll find your match on your local grocery store bulletin board. Just don't put your address, because you don't want anyone dropping by the house and "bugging" or pressuring you. Try to run it as a "blind" ad with just your phone number (your name and address are not identified).

Another way that works virtually every time is to box up unwanted items and some day when it isn't raining, set them out at the curb or street with a big "FREE" sign attached. Chances are, they'll be gone within a day or two. (Take care to anchor contents down so they don't blow away and litter the neighborhood.)

Dealing with Distant Recipients

Never ship anything to an organization without first contacting it to make sure it actually wants the item you wish to donate. This is a particular problem with many groups, such as disaster relief organizations, who find truckloads of clothing arriving for

> Today is a gift. That's why it's called "the present".

months after the disaster is over. Such a well-intentioned mistake costs dearly on both ends. It costs the organization to store or dispose of the goods, and long-distance shipping is very expensive for the donor.

Also, never assume that the unsolicited material will be transported free of charge by the US government or military, private companies or relief organizations. Free shipping is an occasional blessing, but is definitely not the norm.

Shipping Things to Charities Inexpensively

Items may be sent by U.S. Mail (Parcel Post, Media Rate, Library rate or Printed Matter rate), United Parcel Service (UPS), or by motor freight. Simply using the correct category when shipping things via U.S. Mail will result in substantial savings.

There's usually only a few pennies difference between Priority Mail and Parcel Post. If the item is paper, and can go a little slower, take advantage of the three lower "paper" rates. Books can go Media Rate, but if it's books going to a library, they can go library rate, which is lower still. If the items are tracts, or bound material, they can go as "Bound Printed Matter."

A few motor lines will deliver packages free of charge to charitable institutions. Contact some freight companies and ask. If they agree to do so, you will be instructed to mark the packages "DEADHEAD FOR CHARITY" and it will be delivered to the designated charity whenever a truck is going their way, at no charge to you or to the charity. But note that this can only be done if arrangements to do so are made first at the point of origin.

As a general rule, do not send packages by bus or train unless requested to do so by the charity.

God's work done God's way will never lack God's supplies.
-Unknown-

The Landfill: The Disposal of Last Resort

Remember the "homeless" New York City garbage scow that rode the high seas for months looking for someplace to deposit of its load a few years back? Why? All our landfills (all 2,200 of them) are either full or rapidly filling. We've filled in entire cavernous valleys with trash. It is estimated that each year, 1.04 tons of waste is discarded for every citizen of the United States. That's in addition to the 46% of our waste that is now being recycled.

We're not only a consumptive society, we're also a disposable society. We can't wait to get stuff, and then once we do, we throw it out. The sad part is that a large part of the stuff we dispose of could and should be recycled and reused.

The truth is very little trash really is trash. While some people have desperate needs, others are throwing out those exact same needed items. The whole purpose of this book is to help get those goods from those who have them and no longer use them, to those who need them. A secondary benefit is that we'll be making a major contribution toward extending the life of our local landfill.

Our landfills fill up with perfectly good stuff while at the same time, we continue to deplete our resources by manufacturing more of the same stuff

How to Dispose of your Stuff

Chapter Six

SELLING vs. GIVING IT AWAY

Not everyone wants to, or is in a position to give away their belongings when the time comes to dispose of them. Circumstances such as the sudden illness, incapacitation, or loss of a mate may require the sale of certain items to pay hospital, nursing home or funeral expenses, or help the remaining spouse make ends meet or to provide living expenses.

Though this book deals primarily with where to give items, don't let anyone, regardless of how worthy their cause may be, pressure you into donating anything that you don't want to, or don't feel comfortable giving. *A legitimate charity or ministry will not use pressure tactics or try to make you feel guilty if you do not donate.* Don't be rushed into making a donation. Reputable charities are willing to mail you written material describing their programs.

> Common sense is genius dressed in its working clothes.
> - Ralph Waldo Emerson (1803-1882)

Above all, remember, you can't "buy" your way into heaven with good deeds or donations. If you need the proceeds from selling things for your own subsistence, or for paying bills, then selling is definitely the most appropriate thing to do with them. God isn't going to zap you and not let you into Heaven for paying your bills and meeting your obligations. Remember, God's word tells us to "owe no man," so if you need the money to live on, then by all means, sell the stuff.

Ways to Sell Things: Finding Buyers

There are a number of ways to find buyers. But for starters, consider that it might be better to sell items piecemeal. You'll probably realize more money than if you sold the entire household to one buyer. (There are estate buyers who will offer a lump sum for the entire houseful, but they want EVERYTHING, treasures included.) If you're interested in going this route, at least sell off some of the valuables first.

Sell the appliances to a used appliance dealer, the antiques to an antique dealer and then the remainder of the furniture to a used furniture dealer or auction house or sell them yourself via one of the following methods:

Rummage Sales and Garage Sales

One man's trash is another man's treasure.
-unknown-

Whatever the name, — yard sale, estate sale, rummage sale or garage sale, all are a good, fast way to dispose of a variety of goods for ready cash. Little is off limits for selling via such a sale. (Gun sales, for instance, would be prohibited, and there may be local ordinances against certain other items.) But you'll be amazed at what people will buy!

You will find that such sales are popular with rich and poor alike, looking for bargains or something they need or collect. It's also a primary social event for many women. They spend at least one day a week touring local sales. (Imagine the eventual disposal problem *they* are going to have!) There are also "professional" garage sale people, who "buy low and sell high." They're the first buyers arriving at the crack of dawn, snapping up all the bargains, so they can re-sell them later (sometimes even the same day) at their own sales or in their shops.

Pricing

Pricing items correctly is the key to success. The best way to get the feel for pricing is to attend a few local sales yourself and see what percentage of original purchase price things sell for in your area. You might also offer a small fee for a rummage sale "pro" that you meet on your tour, to come price your stuff.

Whatever price you put on items, be prepared to bargain. Don't give things away at sales unless your real objective is to just get rid of everything and the money isn't important, or unless someone who is obviously needy really wants or could use an item, but can't afford it. Then if you feel so led, be a Good Samaritan and give it to that person.

One final word of caution: Try to have a friend or two come help on the day of the sale. Rummage sales are usually too much work for one person, and unless you have eyes in the back of your head, it takes at least one other person to keep an eye on things while the other person acts as cashier.

Hold the sale in the yard or garage, but *lock all doors to the house,* and do not allow anyone access to it. If someone asks to use the bathroom, have your helper escort the person in, wait, and escort him or her out. You don't want to discover later that your personal items in the house grew legs and walked out. Also keep the cash box out of sight and never unattended.

If a rummage sale would be the best option, but you don't want to, or aren't able to do it yourself, call a group you want to donate all or part of the proceeds to, and let them put the sale on for you. This is really worth considering if you end up having to dispose of an estate at a distant point from your home.

One man, having to dispose of his parents' estate on the other side of the country, went back to their homestead and went to a few local rummage sales just to see how things were priced in that area. He had the good fortune to come across a woman who held estate sales professionally, and he hired her.

First she had him go through everything and pick out what he wanted to keep. The next day she showed up with a lot of tables that she set up and covered with all the items. The second day she came back and priced everything. The day of sale, she put out signs, had several women come in and help with the sale. It turned out she was running other sales simultaneously, and customers were directed from sale to sale.

> Economy is the wealth of the poor and the wisdom of the rich.
> -French (on thrift)

By afternoon, virtually everything was sold. When the sale was over, a crew came in and packed up all remaining items (which she got to keep), swept out the entire house, and carried out the trash. The cost for all this service was just 25% of the proceeds (even less in other areas). In just three days she accomplished what it would have taken the son weeks of work and lost wages to accomplish.

In some areas, people who run such sales are listed in the Yellow Pages under "Tag Sale Services."

There's also a franchise called "The Resettlers," that specializes in scale-down moves for older clients. They help plan, pack, unpack and resettle clients in retirement communities and nursing homes, and even operate consignment stores to sell unwanted items. Check your Yellow Pages to see if there's one where you live.

The Lord can clean up the dirtiest of all pots and make it into a beautiful vase
-Unknown-

Flea Markets

Flea markets and many farmers' markets are like giant community rummage sales with all the merchandise sold at a central location instead of at your home.

Each market operates under different rules. Both buyers and sellers usually pay entrance fees. The seller's fee (which may range between $25 to $200 a day) includes the cost of advertising and the space assigned where the selling takes place. Sellers are frequently (but not always) required to supply their own tables and chairs. Flea markets may be indoors or out. If outdoors, sellers may have to provide their own umbrella or canopy for shelter from rain or sun.

The upside is that flea markets are very popular. Those in California are legendary and worth coordinating your vacation plans to coincide with a Saturday in Roseville, San Jose or Santa Barbara. If you sell at a popular flea market, you're practically guaranteed a good crowd.

If possible, attend the one you're thinking of working first to check it out. That will also give you an idea of how to price your items. You might also check your library for Harry Rinker Jr.'s *Price Guide to Flea Market Treasures* (Wallace-Homestead, $19.95).

Also keep an eye open for a flea market dealer who just might want to buy everything you've got. You'll probably get about 40% less for your items, but it will save you the time and effort of selling the stuff yourself.

Be sure to price and tag each item in advance. You won't have time once the sale starts, and even though you can always negotiate and come down in price, a tagged item tells the buyer what you think it is worth for starters.

The downside is that you must haul all your "stuff" to the flea market location (very early in the morning), set it up to display it, sit there all day, and if it doesn't sell, haul it all home again that same day. That's a lot of work!

Auctions

In some parts of the country, auctions are still the preferred way to sell a lot of goods fast. Some are held at auction houses, while in some areas, auctions are still held at the family home. In the latter case, the numbered goods are spread out throughout the house and lawn for preliminary viewing, and then auctioned off by lot.

Saturday auctions are akin to social events, and are frequented by both antique dealers hoping to find a treasure, serious shoppers, and nosy neighbors.

It matters not who does the buying; by nightfall the sale is usually over, the goods are gone to their new homes, the house is empty, and you have your money. Auction house commissions usually run 10% to 15%

ebay (the Internet Auction)

If you have a computer, Internet access and some time to spare, ebay is the biggest on-going garage sale in the world. You can sell ANYTHING on ebay because millions of auctions in over 4,000 cat-

Education is when you read the fine print. Experience is what you get when you don't.
-Pete Seeger-

egories are all going on simultaneously 24-hours a day. A community of 42 million registered buyers and sellers generate $30 million in sales every single day!

What sells? Everything! There's virtually nothing you can think of that wasn't, isn't or won't be listed on ebay.

Even things like pretty old hankies and buttons sell for small fortunes, and at the opposite end of the financial spectrum, big-ticket items like cars, jewels, houses, and timeshares also sell routinely. Now, because of a new partnership with the famed Sotheby's Auction House, high-end arts, antiques, rare books and classic cars will trade owners via ebay too.

It's fun and easy to sell on ebay, not to mention addictive. For those hoping to clean house by selling their excess on ebay, finding buyers isn't the problem. The hard part is not succumbing to buying some other item you've looked for for years (and re-accumulating all over again.)

Even if you don't own a computer, you can still make the whole world your ebay shopping mall by going on-line at your local library (using a free library computer.

Ebay's address is www.ebay.com/

Advertising

Before advertising items for sale, consider the drawbacks. In these days of so much crime, it may not be a good idea to have people come to your house. Criminals have been known to follow the ads, come and take inventory, then come back later to "shop" with no intention of paying.

If you do allow people to come to your home, insist upon an appointment, and make it a point to not be alone when the potential buyers come to the door. You never know who may answer your ad, and each year the newspapers tell horror stories of unsuspecting people who ran ads being robbed, raped, or scammed by supposed "buyers."

If possible, get the name and phone number of people answering the ad who want to come to your house, then later call them back to confirm that they are still coming over. This will verify that they gave you an authentic phone number.

Ask if they will be coming alone. It's very intimidating if a whole group shows up. Not only will you be outnumbered, it's very difficult to keep track of more than two or three people. It's been known to happen that while one person keeps the seller occupied, others in the group can slip off and steal things elsewhere in the house. If possible, walk them out to the car, and memorize or make note of their license number before they leave. If anything turns up missing later, the police will have a definite starting point of whom to look for.

When advertising, it pays to call around and compare ad prices first. Even small ads in big metropolitan papers are expensive. A local neighborhood paper may be cheaper, but will only reach a tiny handful of people. A regional "Little Nickel" or "Thrifty Shopper" may actually reach a larger audience at the same or lower cost. Before spending money on multiple insertions, list specific items in one ad, and see how they sell. The next week, advertise another selection of things. Those who call to inquire about one item usually ask what else you have.

Learn from the mistakes of others. You can't live long enough to make them all yourself. -Unknown-

If holding an actual "sale," on the day of the sale, make it easy to find your house. If it's legal to put signs on phone poles in your area, put posters with the words "SALE" or "GARAGE SALE" and an arrow, pointing the way to the big event. Be sure to print legibly and use large size dark letters that can be read from a moving car.

For genuine objects d'art, it may pay to take out an ad in a specialty publication such as *Antiques & the Arts Weekly*. A one-column ad will run about $10.00 (203-426-8036). The same holds true for other big-ticket items. Advertise a car in your local Car & Truck Trader, for example, because a photo of the vehicle will be included in the price of the ad (usually about $25.00).

39

Consignment

There are consignment shops for many items you will be disposing of: clothing shops, antique consignors, auto consignors and auto auctions, children's consignment shops, plus furniture and appliance consignors. They will take your items, put them in their store, and pay you your share when they sell.

Be sure to get the agreement in writing, clearly spelling out what percentage each of you gets, and what happens to the items after a certain amount of time if they don't sell. Are they to be returned to you, donated to charity, or kept by the consignee? If donated to charity, specify that *you* get the tax receipt. After all, you are the donor, not the consignee.

Also be sure the agreement specifies exactly when you are to be paid, such as within 48 hours of sale, within 7 days of sale, or by the first of the following month after the sale. Be aggressive in collecting if your payment doesn't show up exactly when due. Some people have a problem in parting with other people's money once they have their hands on it. They start rationalizing to themselves as to why they are entitled to keep it all.

Good memories are our second chance at happiness.
-Queen Elizabeth-

Chapter Seven

DETERMINING WHO GETS WHAT

One of the saddest chapters in many a family's history is that of relationships broken up by disputes and lawsuits over inheritances. Many times the battles are over moderately valued items. The last thing most parents want is for their children and heirs to become acrimonious and litigious over material goods.

> Skill is fine, and genius is splendid, but right contacts are more valuable than either.
> -Archibald McIndoe-

If the planning is done in advance, there are several ways to help avoid this.

The "up front" Method: Ask descendants and heirs (in descending order of relationship) which of your items they would like to inherit. Chances are they already have a wish list. Have them make a prioritized list, and tell them you will consider all their requests and that you are attempting to see that each person get at least one of their top choices. (With a little luck, not everyone will want the same items.)

The problem, of course, is that while sentimental daughter Amy may covet the old willow rocker Grandpa made as a boy, daughter Suzy may want Grandma's 4-carat diamond. Even if each daughter is content with the disparity in monetary value, chances are good that Amy's descendants may go through life feeling that their Grandma Amy got short-changed.

One way would be to try to equalize the value each "layer" of inheritors gets. (This method should probably only be utilized for material items, not real estate, since it would be much harder to try to equalize parcels of land and buildings.) Once the designated items are allotted, they should all be clearly itemized in the will. Better still, spell out the disbursals in separate written instructions. Then if the list changes, the will doesn't have to be redrafted.

Some people also like to write a family letter announcing who will be inheriting what. Knowledge that the whole family is informed in advance as to what will belong to each person can frequently avert an unscrupulous member coming in upon the death of the testator to make a premature "dispersal" and having the choice items disappear.

2. In the case of really valuable family heirlooms, many "next" generational battles may be averted by skipping a generation and leaving the items to someone in the third or even fourth generation. In other words, leave the old family music box to Daughter Amy's granddaughter Betsy, even though Betsy may only be a baby. The stipulation must be added that the music box is to stay in the care of Amy and later Betsy's mother until baby Betsy is a responsible adult, gets married, or graduates from college, or whatever other stipulations you wish to impose.

> "You have not lived until you have done something for someone who can never repay you."
> -John Bunyan-
> (1628-88)

That way, daughter Amy (generation 2) and Betsy's mother (generation 3) get many years of use and enjoyment out of it too, without the resentment of their other children for giving it to Betsy. Grandma (you) made that decision, not Amy or Betsy's mother.

3. All large assets, such as the family home, other real estate, company businesses, etc., are definitely part of your estate. Disposal of those should be decided only after discussing the various options with your attorney.

4. Another option to seriously consider, is passing along valued items to heirs while you are still alive. If you're no longer using your Sterling silverware with service for twelve, your silver coffee service, a big piece of valuable furniture or a nice item of jewelry, why not pass it along *now* and have the satisfaction of watching the recipient enjoy it?

Remember how often you've heard older people say they wished people would send them flowers while they were still alive, instead of sending them to their funerals? Well that works in reverse too. Give away nice items you no longer use now, and watch someone else get the same pleasure of ownership that you did.

The Common Mistake We all Make

When asked what most people intend to do with all their belongings, the most common answer is, "we're going to leave it all to our children." The kids meanwhile are dreading the thought of the monumental task they're going to inherit. If the truth were known, there are probably only a few of our items they would really like to have.

This was illustrated by a story told by a couple we met who took a long-planned trip to Europe and searched high and low for a really great souvenir for their daughter.

They finally found something they were convinced she would really love and treasure. It was a gorgeous wine decanter, 2-1/2 feet high with hand-wrought iron grape leaves entwined around it. They lovingly hand carried their treasure all over Europe throughout the rest of their trip, and finally managed to get it home safely.

Their daughter graciously accepted it, and after an appropriate time… quietly put it in a garage sale.

Another lady we know has a vast collection of rare and valuable antiques. She sadly told us her daughter has no interest in them, and her son-in-law wouldn't allow them in his house. Forget the fact the antiques are worth a million dollars. To him, they're just "old clutter."

The fact that's hard to face, is that our children may have tastes totally opposite of our own.

Another reality is that many of today's younger generation earn more than their parents ever dreamed of earning. Parents growing up in the depression era frequently grew up with a "poor" mentality. Even as they eventually acquired things, they hung onto the old things, thinking that one day they would be "helping" their children by passing on the goods. But as the children got married, the old "dowry" was obsolete, old-fashioned or unwanted.

If you don't have a plan for yourself, you'll be a part of someone else's.

43

The safest route is two-fold. Don't assume your children will welcome "everything" or even anything you've got. ASK them to tell you specifically what they DO and DO NOT want, and then start now to dispose of the rest.

FAMILY TREASURES

These are items whose value may be more sentimental than monetary, and if at all possible, they should remain within the family.

One local newspaper editor wrote an insightful column describing how she rethought her strategy of what family treasures she would try to save in the event of a fire.

Like most of us, she originally thought the most precious thing would be to save the family photo album. Then she realized that there already were copies of most of her photos since her grown children already had their own photo albums with duplicates of hers, and the photos were replaceable.

That freed her up to get down to the irreplaceable treasures.

Her "things to save first" list was then revised to start with Grandpa's 100 year-old oak rocking chair, and great-grandma's antique washbowl and pitcher.

Make a list of your most valuable family treasures and start thinking about who should inherit them.

Antiques are things one generation buys, the next generation gets rid of, and the following generation buys again.

The Family Bible

It used to be, and in many areas still is, a tradition to record the vital statistics of all family members ((births, deaths and marriages) in the family Bible. The job of making entries was akin to a sacred trust. In the case of a dispute over a date, the date in the family Bible would take precedence over word of mouth, newspaper articles, and even government records (since up until this century, many such "outside" records may not have been recorded for weeks or even months after the event).

As long as there are any descendants still living, the family Bible should be passed on to whichever of the following is the most responsible and apt to keep it up. This could be the oldest son, the closest sister to the deceased, a meticulous aunt, the family genealogist, or the most detail-oriented person in the family.

If there are no family descendants, such as in the case of the end of a bloodline, consider giving the bible to a library (state, genealogy, or local.)

Thanks to our now living in the age of technology, you could also have someone with Internet access go on-line and post a message with one of the genealogy services or chat groups that the Bible is available, and ask if someone from another branch of the family would like it. It will almost certainly find a taker.

> To what greater inspiration and course can we turn than to the imperishable truth to be found in this treasure house, - the Bible.
> -Queen Elizabeth II-

The Old Family Photo Album

To a genealogist, a clearly identified and dated old photo is equal to a gold nugget. It is a rare window through which you can see someone in your past. With today's technology, photos can be scanned onto a computer disk so every family member can be given his or her own disk and make their own copies. However, not everyone cares about the family heritage, so the most logical recipient is the family member who is the most interested.

If there is no family genealogist, or no one cares to become one, old photos may be of interest to the state, county or local historical society, library, genealogy society, or a local private historian. Although it would be hard for an individual to find a buyer for a nondescript old photo album, there are buyers out there. Thrift stores put a pretty high price on them, and it doesn't take long for them to be gone.

One thing that infinitely increases the value of old photos is the identification of the subjects. Even if you can't identify everyone in your photos, make it a goal to go through them and identify as many people as possible *NOW!* Have other relatives try to identify unknowns too. Your descendants will be grateful!

There's one other problem to keep in mind. Be sure that the person who inherits the family photos has a sharing nature. How sad when an album falls into the hands of someone selfish who treats it as their own private property, instead of allowing the entire family to share and get to see their ancestors. This also holds true for family genealogies. Unfortunately it does happen.

Diaries

While some folks keep diaries for eventual public consumption, most are private; and most writers would be embarrassed to think that someday strange and prying eyes were reading their innermost thoughts.

If the writer is still alive, he/she should consider the ultimate disposition of the diaries in advance and make arrangements for them. If you don't want them read until well after your death, you might seal them in a strongbox, and will it to an infant descendent with instructions that the box is not to be opened until the infant's 40th birthday (or any date you pick). You might tuck in a hundred-dollar bill or two or some other little treasure to reward them for their patience.

If you are disposing of someone else's diaries, unless the deceased died a sudden death, assume the writer would want his or her closest descendants to receive it. If disposing of your own diary, is your mate still alive? If not, then perhaps leave it to children in descending birth order, or to one in the next generation.

If the diary belonged to a historic figure, or if the contents contain detailed historical accounts (e.g., diaries of people who traveled over the Oregon Tail, or were the first settlers in an area), perhaps a historical society would be a worthy and appreciative recipient.

What is a diary as a rule? A document useful to the person who keeps it. Dull to the contemporary who reads it and invaluble to the student, centuries afterwards, who treasures it.
-Helen Terry-

Scrapbooks

Scrapbooks are usually sentimental repositories. They contain things like dance programs, invitations, notes, newspaper clippings, old valentines and scraps of this and that, which seldom mean much except to the person who saved them.

They may, however, be quite valuable to the family genealogist because they might put specific dates on newsworthy events.

Some of those mementos may actually be quite valuable too. For instance, things like old Disneyland "A" tickets bring a pretty price from collectors and souvenirs from the 1933 World's Fair are also rate commodities. Even the entire scrapbook, intact, would probably be a saleable item on ebay, the world biggest Internet auction.

Baby Books, from when the family grew by two feet

Baby Books and Childhood Mementos

The bible says there comes a time to put away childish things. If you haven't already given their baby books, old school papers, artwork, and other child-hood mementos to the "babies" (who may now be parents or grandparents themselves), this is the time to do it.

Actually those childish papers might have some interesting tales to tell. Perhaps little Harry's early draw-ings or writings showed he had a particular talent or proclivity toward certain things. If Harry's first drawing was of a car, and Harry now owns an auto dealer-ship, Harry's company might appreciate having that drawing framed in the boardroom or executive suite. If Suzie's early drawing pictured her as a nurse, and she's now a hospital administrator, she too might want to add that paper to her accumulation.

If Harry and Suzie don't want their childhood trea-sures, perhaps their present-day children or grand-children might. Most kids find it hard to imagine that the older generation was ever as young as them-selves, and what better way to prove that they were, than to produce the written "evidence" of grandpa or grandma's art work or school papers. The youngsters of today are usually impressed when they see how much better penmanship was in the "old" days. It might even inspire them to come up to grandpa's standards.

The most valuable item in those baby books, aside from the memories, may be those cute little locks of hair containing junior's DNA. Of course if you're like some adoring parents, you've saved enough baby trimmings to build a whole new baby. But if you haven't already done so, this is the time to transfer all pertinent data about all children into a good computer genealogy program, and be sure to note where those little locks of hair are kept before passing the baby books on.

Family Recipes

An army may travel on its stomach, but just about every family has grown up on some woman's cooking. Everyone has fond memories of some wonderful dish from their childhood. Many families, in fact, look upon prized old family recipes as part of the family's "wealth" which should be passed on from mother to daughter. They compile their most treasured recipes into coveted handwritten cookbooks (which are frequently called "Dowry Cookbooks.")

Whether this is a tradition in your family or not, think what a marvelous legacy it would be to put those favorite old recipes in writing so future generations can actually taste them. Great-grandma Jones' Christmas pudding, or Grandpa Henry's sourdough pancakes could still be replicated decades, or even centuries from now if you write them down. The only thing better would be a compilation of *many* family members' favorite recipes that could then be copied and distributed to the whole clan. With the capabilities of computers now readily available, it would be a simple matter to make a disc or printouts of the family cookbook.

In addition, many cooks have keepsake cookbooks they reference for much of their cooking. Some are commercially published, some collected from

My mother's menu consisted of two choices:

Take it or leave it.

-Buddy Hackettcharitable or social organizations, and some are ethnic collections. Younger cooks who grew up loving the recipes would prize these books.

The Family Genealogy

If fortunate enough to be the keeper of the family genealogy, one of your very top priorities should be to see that your thousands of hours of hard work were not spent in vain, once you join the army of ancestors. No sadder words were ever uttered than "My grandmother worked on the family tree for years, but after she died, my mom threw it all out!"

Assuming your "line" has not died out, start with your own family, and see if any other member is interested in taking over. If not, how about another branch of the family?

Still no luck? How about one of the young people in the family? It may take a little educational effort. (Rent a copy of the Roots video and show it to them). Take them to a genealogy fair. If you have interesting early American roots, take them back to the homestead or walk the streets of the towns where the ancestors lived.

Go look at the old home sites and graveyards. Look in local libraries and show them records and stories of great-great grandma and grandpa. In other words, bring history alive to them. Make it a fun, fascinating adventure that all relates to them personally. Get them hooked!

Pay them to do a little research. Check the Internet to see if there are any other distant relatives their age that might already be interested in genealogy. It might be even more fun with a pen pal.

Still no takers? Don't give up. There are a variety of "outside" sources that would love to have your research and papers.

Check with your local library, archives and/or university to see if they want it. Many don't have the staff to process someone's family history, however if it has strong local or historic interest they may jump at the chance to get it.

I think that I shall never see a completed genealogy

—Unknown

The largest repository of genealogical matter in the U.S. is the Mormon Church, and they have information on virtually everybody, Mormon and non-Mormon alike.

Contact the Family History Library at your local Mormon Church or write or call directly to Salt Lake City to the mother lode of all genealogy repositories: Family History Library, Church of Jesus Christ of Latter Day Saints, 35 North West Temple Street, Salt Lake City, UT 84150-3400. Phone (801) 240-2331.

Also check with The Genealogical Center Library, Box 88100, Atlanta, GA 30356-8100. Chances are good they'll want everything you've got! This is the only genealogical library in the U.S. that provides services for the blind and handicapped. They also provide a low-cost book loan program for the general public. They have a Family Group File, where family group sheets are filed alphabetically for patrons to use. They have the equipment to microfilm and preserve your notes and files. If you live near Atlanta, they can always use more file cabinets, typewriters, computers, microfilm readers, etc.

Another (smaller) library that welcomes donations of genealogy papers and books is Fiske Genealogical Foundation, 1644 - 43rd Avenue East, Seattle, WA 98112-3222. (206) 328-2716.

Before giving away any genealogy records, be sure everything is clearly marked. Put title pages on your binders and notebooks, noting what's inside. Put a copy of your pedigree chart in the front, and circle whatever family is included in this file.

Genealogists live in the past lane.

-Unknown-

For works in progress, get some 9 x 12 envelopes, write the family surname on the front, and put all notes and scraps in the envelopes. File them in alphabetical order.

For unrecorded and uncategorized material such as letters, birth and death certificates, census records, pages copied from books, etc., put them in a box marked UNRECORDED GENEALOGY.

Make sure all file folders are clearly labeled, photos are identified, and things such as letters are marked as to who they're from, and their relationship. Ideally, a stranger should be able to come in and figure out your system and find things in your files. Someday someone may have to.

If you want any of your material typed or published or otherwise distributed to various libraries, be sure you leave money in your will for that to be done. Finally, be sure to put a codicil in your will providing for the disposition of your genealogical materials and equipment. If you want your books, magazines and newsletters to go to one organization, your pedigree charts and family group sheets to another, and your equipment to another, be sure to spell that out clearly in the codicil.

One final word. As with family photos, pick a recipient who is not grasping. We know of one man who spent thousands of hours compiling his family genealogy. He even traveled to England to do research, but as fate would have it, died there while researching. To this day, his wife will not share any of his findings with his family, the very people he was doing it for. Sadder still is that as time goes by, his family members are dying off without ever getting to enjoy the fruits of his labor.

If you don't know [your family's] history, then you don't know anything. You are a leaf that doesn't know it is part of a tree.

-Michael Crichton-

Family Oral History

If time, energy and circumstances permit, gather together all the younger members of the family, and spend a few hours telling old family history, stories and anecdotes, showing pictures from old photo albums, relating a little oral history such as when and how the original ancestors came to America, and cap the event off with a feast or cooking demonstration of old family food favorites.

The very act of preparing for such an event will dredge up many long forgotten stories (make notes as they come to mind) and be as rewarding for the "old-timer" as it is for the family. (What "old timer" doesn't like to tell stories of his youth? It will also be perhaps the greatest thing you can do for the children to give them a sense of "family," lineage continuity, and history as it relates to them.

Tell about things from your younger days, things like soda fountains, juke boxes, candy cigarettes, party lines, phone numbers with word prefixes, wringer washers, War Bonds and dime US Savings Stamps, fifteen cent McDonald hamburgers, penny postcards, penny candy and 25-cent-a gallon gasoline. Tell how much it cost to buy your first home, or what's now the family homestead (probably not much more than it costs for one house payment for many of today's homes.)

A Saturday matinee was a dime, and that was a lot of money in the good old days, and the hospital bill for going in and having a baby was $40, and mom stayed for a week.

Many a young person has gotten a whole new appreciation of history when they realize that his or her own flesh and blood ancestors were actually a part of it. Remember to tell stories about their parents when they were little. Most children can't imagine their parents as children, and they love to hear funny stories about mom and dad.

As you tell the stories, weave in family traditions, such things as why you open Christmas presents on Christmas eve instead of Christmas Day, or why certain foods are served on birthdays, or how certain family traditions came about.

When you talk about births, marriages and deaths in the family, be sure to list any dates and places that you know. Also be sure to discuss maiden names and married names. Some future genealogist will bless you for it.

Of utmost importance is to keep a tape recorder (or better still) video camera handy and running, and be sure to get the old stories and recollections *recorded!* (Keep in mind however, that the shelf life of video tape and audio tape is limited. When time permits, transcribe the tape or find a more permanent storage medium.)

Every life has a story.

-A&E Biography-

One "latter day" innovation to consider is to create a family web page. The young people in the family will know how to do it, and it will do wonders toward giving them a sense of family.

Family Memorabilia

Every family has a few certain items that fall into that strange category between antique value and sentimental value. It may not be a pretty or unique item, but it was part of a wonderful story or perhaps was part of a family tradition. It may be an item that's always brought out at Christmas time, or perhaps it is only used at weddings. Whatever it is, keep it within the family. Place it with the person most apt to appreciate it and keep the legend, tradition, or history alive and on going.

Grandma's Wedding Gown

The least used, but longest-kept item of clothing in every woman's wardrobe is usually her wedding gown. She wears it once, but keeps it forever. (Sadly, about 50% of the gowns outlast the marriages, these days.)

A lovely tradition one Ohio family practices, is for the wedding dress to be given a few more trips down the aisle by other family females - sisters, daughters, nieces, aunts, granddaughters, etc. So far, the women of the family have used "Mom's wedding dress" ten times in the last couple decades. Each user alters it for length and fit, and by use of different veils, flower arrangements and headdresses, modifies it to the tastes of the wearer. Use of "the Gown" is now such a tradition in that family, no future bride would consider wearing anything else.

Not only would this be a fun tradition for a family to adopt, it would save a small fortune for the bride's parents, the newlyweds, or whomever pays for the wedding. New wedding gowns these days cost from hundreds to thousands of dollars.

"Memories, important yesterdays, were once todays. Treasure and notice today." - Gloria Gaither-

If you'd like to donate the gown to a worthy cause, *Making Memories Breast Cancer Foundation*, a Portland, Oregon-based charity, sells gently-used wedding dresses and uses the proceeds to grant wishes to men (yes, men) and women who have metastasis breast cancer. Their address is:

Making Memories Breast Cancer Foundation
12708 SE Stephens Street,
Portland, OR 97233
(503) 252-3955.

The gift of the gown is 100% deductible as is the postage. They ask that you put your name and address on the inside of the box as well as on the outside to aid them in getting your receipt to you. They also ask that you include a $5 donation to help with the cost of cleaning and processing the gown.

Bridesmaid Dresses

First a bridesmaid dress, then a gown for the belle of the ball.

Even bridesmaid dresses can be transformed into Cinderella ball gowns! The Glass Slipper Project, a Chicago-based charity, accepts donations of evening wear and accessories to distribute to disadvantaged high school girls to wear at their proms. Dresses must be in current style, excellent or almost-new condition, and clean. They can also use matching shoes, gloves, jewelry, new unopened makeup, unopened hosiery and home styling hair kits. They especially need gowns size 16 or larger.

This group is listed on page 216 under clothing.

Many senior centers or nursing homes can use formal wear for their residents to wear to their "Senior Proms" or other festive formal events. There's also the annual "Bridesmaids' Ball" in Philadelphia, a fun charity event, where bridesmaids compete to win the "Worst Dress" contest. Proceeds from ticket and ad sales are used to support the Leukemia and Lymphoma Society

Something Old, Something New

Other wedding "accouterments" which are good prospects for becoming family traditions and passing on, are engagement and wedding rings, garters, lingerie, bridal veils, gloves, purses and wedding bibles.

Heirlooms and Antiques

Antiques should be treated as part of the estate. Got an item you aren't sure of? If in doubt, check it out. Set aside any items that may be antiques, and get the opinion of a respected antique dealer or appraiser (about $100 an hour). Look in the Yellow Pages under "Appraisers" or call the American Society of Appraisers (800-272-8258) for names of appraisers in your area. Your library will also probably have antiques price guides. It's also possible to check the value of virtually anything by doing an Internet search.

It's prudent to never get rid of anything until you have an unbiased professional come in and take a look at what you have and give you an opinion.

Items that have been in the family a long time should stay within the family. Even if they aren't valued as antiques, they may still have historical or sentimental value to the descendants or other family members.

Questions antique dealers and/or appraisers may have are:

- the approximate age of the piece
- where or when it was purchased (if known)
- any recollection of previous owners (to help identify its age or origin)
- where it was made (geographic identification)
- when it came into the family
- when first obtained, was it new or used?
- has it been repaired, refurbished or refinished?

children look upon old family heirlooms as ugly and corny, but as adults they covet and treasure them.

Once the valuable items are disposed of, consider giving other old items no family member shows an interest in, to appropriate historical societies or museums.

Diamonds & Gems, Gold & Other Precious Metals

Gemstones and precious metals are obviously valuable, whether they are made into jewelry or not. Most heirs would appreciate receiving them, whatever state they're in. When deciding on diamond recipients, don't forget young males in the family. While such an inheritance might not be fully appreciated at a tender age, it certainly would be when the time comes the young man wants to get engaged. If in the unlikely event nobody does want them, look in the Yellow Pages under "Jewelers", "Jewelry Buyers", "Jewelry Designers" or "Diamond Buyers" for potential buyers.

Old gold dental caps, partials, bridges or crowns may be converted into cash by looking in the Yellow Pages under Gold, Silver and Platinum Buyers or calling 1-800-WE-BUY-GOLD (1-800-93-289-4653) for a free dental and broken gold recycling kit. (That's Lippincott Incorporated, 1001 City Avenue, P. O. Box 578, Wynnewood, PA 19096-0578). They also buy old chains, school rings, wedding bands, earrings, and any other item that may contain gold or precious metals.

A diamond is a piece of coal that finished what it started.
-Unknown-

Silverware

If you choose to sell your sterling silver pieces and silverware instead of passing them on to heirs, there are a number of companies who buy entire services, or just a piece or two. Get bids for your pieces from several buyers before shipping off the pieces. It may pay to photograph them first before shipping too.

Some companies to check with are:

Atlantic Silver
7405 NW 57th St.
Tamarac, FL 33319
1-800-288-6665

Silver Queen
730 N. Indian Rocks Road
Bellfair Bluffs, FL 33770
1-800-262-3134

Beverly Bremer Silver Shop
3164 Peachtree Road
Atlanta, GA 30305

Marks China, Crystal and Silverware
315 Franklin Avenue
Wycoff, NJ 07481
1-800-862-7578

Walter Drake
Drake Building
Colorado Springs, CO 80940

> **The more sand that has escaped from the hourglass of our life, the clearer we should see through it.**
>
> **-Jean Paul Sartre-**

Grandfather, Mantle and Anniversary Clocks

These fall into the heirloom category, and should stay within the family if at all possible. Consider skipping a generation, and giving it to a grandchild who shows an appreciation for fine things.

Remember that wonderful old song about the Grandfather Clock, and when you give the clock, give it complete with a recitation or *written* synopsis about all the family events the clock has been through or a part of. It might be fun to write it as if it were the clock speaking and telling stories of events that have taken place since it became part of the household.

Inexpensive Clocks and Watches

All residents of group homes can use clocks and watches. Their special needs might dictate which type of timepiece might be most appropriate for them. Many residents of homes for the developmentally disabled and/or the retarded can use only digital watches, since they can understand them, but frequently can't tell time with a conventional analog timepiece.

Lots of groups can use alarm clocks: any facility with live-in residents, camps, schools, prisons, or halfway houses. Being on time may mean the difference

**Time is something
everyone runs
short on and
finally runs out of.**

between getting hired and keeping a job for someone coming off welfare, or working for the first time. Those in Senior Centers might appreciate those clocks and watches with large, easy-to-read faces.

Chapter Eight

PERSONAL ITEMS

Clothing

Most of the closets in America are full of clothes that are either too small or too large. The truth is, most of us live in just a few favorite items of clothing. Meanwhile, our closets are packed with clothes we'll never wear again. Written into our closets are our personal histories of the Battle of the Bulge.

Start by getting rid of your "fat clothes." Many people, who ever had a weight problem and succeeded in dropping a few pounds, still keep a wardrobe of "fat clothes." They keep them "just in case" they may someday need them again. The truth is, oversize clothes are a "crutch" to fall back upon. Burn that bridge, and tell yourself "I'll NEVER pass this way again." If you must keep something, pick just one piece, the WORST, biggest and ugliest item, just to remind yourself how badly you looked at one time. Then you really never will pass this way again.

The opposite problem is all those clothes we bought to "grow into." These are the little beauties (many still wearing their price tags) that have never been worn since the day they were purchased.

Meanwhile, both the "fat" clothes and the "skinny" clothes just grow old together, more out of style, and do nothing but collect dust, feed moths, and fill up the closet. Take a deep breath and attack the closet ruthlessly.

If you're disposing of someone else's estate, never discard a deceased person's clothing without first checking all pockets and seams. People have been known to secret wads of cash in various coat, jacket and dress pockets and old handbags. (While you're at it, also play detective and look in other places money or jewels might have been hidden such as in or under a mattress, inside a china sugar bowl stored away in the china cupboard, or frozen in ice cube

> God won't ask about the clothes you had in your closet, but He'll ask how many you helped to clothe.
> -Unknown-

trays. Had these items been disposed of without first being checked, some recipients down the line would have been in for a pleasant surprise.

Many churches have made arrangements for the distribution of clothing, shoes, blankets and coats to people in need or victims of some calamity. Homeless shelters also need a continual supply of clothing and shoes.

Sort clothes according to age and quality. Very old clothes or dated clothes may be of interest to museums and little theater groups.

Remember too, any organization that takes clothes can probably also use rolling clothing racks, shelving or garment bags and storage units.

Who NOT to Give Clothes to

When professional disaster responders get together, one of their usual topics are the horror stories about "second disasters."

"What is a "second disaster"? It is the deluge of inappropriate used clothing that pours into a disaster area after a major calamity. With news of every devastating tornado, hurricane, flood, wildfire, or other disaster, it isn't long before the influx starts. It isn't uncommon to hear that emergency vehicles have been hampered by tractor-trailers full of mixed unsorted clothing, food, tools, and (no kidding) junk, wrestling for right of way.

If you would give yourself a blessing, give to others what you yourself would like to have.

The first problem is usually that there is nobody to even begin to sort the containers. It takes a crew of 20 experienced sorters three whole days to unload, sort and prepare one semi truck. What volunteers are available usually are busy helping survivors, looking for lost family members, and seeing to immediate needs.

The second problem is that when there finally is time to start to look over the contents, what is frequently found is perishable rotting food, wet and mildewing or molding clothes full of fleas and mites, broken household appliances or those with missing parts, and mountains of unmatched shoes. Plus tons of just plain junk and inappropriate clothing. What are people thinking of to send evening gowns, high heeled shoes and fake fur coats to people who have just had their homes flooded out or destroyed.

The sad part is, most of these donations come from good-hearted, well-intentioned people. It usually starts when a radio station puts out the call for donations, and everyone rushes to clean out their closet.

Disaster responders offer the following advice: If you really want to help out following an emergency, call FEMA or one of the voluntary disaster responders: Salvation Army, Church World Service Disaster Response Office, Adventist Community Service (ACS), Lutheran Disaster Response and Northwest Medical Teams International, and ask what their "needs list" contains. They ask that if any item has not been specifically responded, please DO NOT send it.

> I have never heard anything about the resolutions of the apostles, but a great deal about their acts.
> -Horace Mann-

What is usually REALLY needed following a disaster, is bottled water, Pedialyte, cleaning materials, chain saws, electric generators, truckloads of wheelbarrows and tools, sheets, blankets, mosquito nets, and underwear, especially children's underwear. Following Hurricane Andrew, the Adventists sent in 10,000 pairs of size 5 underwear. Why? Because children often regress after a disaster, even losing their potty training. With no water available, every day, disaster responders are burning dirty underwear, and needing replacements.

Most compassionate people would rather fill a box than write a check. (9-11 was an exception), but the above organizations really do put those dollars to the purpose you intend. They get $175 worth of goods for every dollar donated, thanks in part to generous manufacturers.

They also use the money to give cash vouchers to victims to meet immediate emergency needs to buy what they need most. This is one time we do advocate giving cash.

The addresses of the above organizations are all listed on page 221.

Professional Dress Clothes

Don't spend two dollars to dry clean a shirt. Donate it to the Salvation Army instead. They'll clean it and put it on a hanger. Next morning buy it back for seventy-five cents.

-Billiam Coronel-

If you have some nice professional suits to dispose of, don't forget "Dress for Success." This not-for-profit organization helps low-income women make tailored transitions into the workforce. Each Dress for Success client receives one suit when she has a job interview, and a second suit when she gets the job.

Many *Dress for Success* affiliates actually provide more than just those two suits. They give extra items like silk scarves, blouses and other interview-appropriate clothing items. Their goal is to provide a sharp-looking interview suit to help land the job, and then enough items to mix-and-match for a whole week's worth of work attire.

Women are referred to dress for Success by other not-for-profits and government agencies including homeless shelters, domestic violence shelters, immigration services and job training programs. Dress for Success provides interview suits, confidence boosts and career development to more than 30,000 women in over 70 cities each year.

Warm Clothing

In some parts of the country, the gift of warmth is the gift of life. Blankets, warm coats, mittens, gloves, heavy wool socks, warm long underwear, wool pants and winter boots could mean the difference between comfort and misery to many impoverished people.

Many cities have missions, ministries and outreach groups that gather supplies for such people, while in other areas, you may have to search out the recipients for yourself. If the latter is the case, ask the visiting nurse service if they know of anyone needing blankets and warm clothing. Salvation Army or a Union Gospel Mission may distribute them for you.

If you want to help the homeless personally, arrange to have some men from your church or synagogue take the goods in a box and leave them under a bridge where homeless people are known to live, or leave them in the doorway of a building they are known to inhabit.

Fur Coats

Furs are a quandary. Some furriers still buy quality used fur coats to take them apart and remake them into modern styles.

If you can't find a buyer, another use for vintage fur is reincarnate it into handmade teddy bears, or a nice warm throw or blanket. There are many bear makers out there who would be happy to make it into cute critters for a price.

Some handsome mink teddy bears or bunnies made from grandma's vintage coat would be heirlooms that would be treasured for several more generations.

A friend by your side can keep you warmer than the richest furs

Kid Stuff

They may be little people, but in no time, even tiny ones soon accumulate a lot of "stuff." They have special furniture, clothes food, toys, and "equipment."

Unlike their adult family members, children quickly grow through sizes and gear, and unless more children are anticipated in the family, there are always many needs recipients for good baby and small child accouterments.

Many churches with nurseries can use spare cribs, booster seats, and small furniture. So can battered women shelters, refugee services, homes for unwed mothers, and low-income day care centers.

Child car seats can be given to local fire departments. Many keep them on hand for loaners.

Baby and Children's Clothing

Nearly every city has a home that cares for babies born drug or alcohol addicted, HIV positive, and/or babies that are neglected, abandoned or abused. Call the Women's Editor at your local newspaper for local groups that run such homes.

Children's clothes can also be used by shelters for abused women. Battered women and their children frequently leave home with just the clothes on their backs.

Shoes

Missions and those who work with the homeless always need sturdy men's shoes, while women's shoes can be used by domestic abuse shelters. The latter can also use children's shoes.

Especially valuable are work shoes, warm boots, and sturdy high top boots. Many jobs require working outdoors in the worst of weather, and it's sad but true that when your feet get cold, you're cold all over.

Most churches like to keep a supply of all kinds and sizes of shoes since churches are frequently the first line of supply for local needs.

Odd Shoes

In 1940, a unique "shoe" organization was founded to service polio survivors. Today N.O.S.E. (National Odd Shoe Exchange) continues to provide the "odd" shoe needed by amputees or people with odd sizes.

If the shoe fits, wear it (or give it to someone who can)

Footwear must be new, unworn and undamaged. National Odd Shoe Exchange accepts matched pairs, pairs, singles and bulk footwear items. (Shoes, boots, slippers, etc.) All sizes and styles are needed. N.O.S.E. cannot accept worn or damaged items. They can also use socks, inserts, orthotics, laces, office supplies, packaging materials, promotional items, warehouse equipment and office equipment.

National Odd Shoe Exchange
3200 North Delaware Street
Chandler, AZ 85225-1000
Telephone: (480) 892-3484 FAX (480) 892-3568

Old Sneakers

Even used tennis shoes can avoid the local landfill. Some stores that sell nothing but athletic shoes accept them for recycling. The shoes are ground up in a tire grinder, and the resulting chips are called "Sneaker Chips." The chips are then used for playground padding and running tracks.

One such store is "The Foot Zone in Seattle (206) 329-1466 or (425) 556-0383. Some Niketown stores also accept them.

Costumes

Little theater groups, or schools which teach drama or have productions would probably welcome old costumes, in fact, the older the better. Perhaps your local high school or university could use them if they do theatrical productions (and have storage space).

Suitcases

Suitcases, backpacks, valises, fanny packs, duffle bags and footlockers can be used by any number of people. Such people range from the homeless, inner-city kids going to camp, runaway teens, "street-people" and entire families who live in alleys, parks and under bridges.

The suitcases can be left at missions, shelters, run-away teen centers, youth-camp sponsors or churches that minister to such folks.

Umbrellas, Rain Gear and Goulashes

Rain gear is a valuable commodity to many groups: the homeless, persons (including children) who must stand out in weather waiting for busses, campers, scouts, those who live in institutions with a spread-out "campus" (such as residential institutions where residents must travel between cottages or dormitories and classrooms.)

Churches are the first places many needy people turn for help, and most maintain clothing closets to help those with an emergency. Rain gear is one of the things they can always use more of.

> If a farmer fills his barn with grain, he gets mice. If he leaves it empty, he gets actors.
> -Bill Vaughan-

Chapter Nine

More WOMEN'S THINGS

Cosmetics

Some cosmetics can be used by others, some cannot. Oil or grease-based makeup items should be discarded since they could harbor germs or bacteria. These include lipsticks which have been used, pancake makeup, creams which can go rancid and used deodorant.

The "safe" ones are powders (provided the powder puff is new), new lipsticks, makeup, bottled moisturizers, foundations, nail polish, skin freshener, and perfumes.

Ladies who might need and appreciate such goods are those in domestic abuse centers, women's prisons, and homes for the retarded.

Costume Jewelry

Today's faux jewelry is so good, if you aren't the original purchaser of the object in question, you may not know whether you're holding a real gem or an imitation. Many jewelers will give you "unofficial" appraisals and ballpark estimates of value for no charge. For estate purposes, you would probably need an "official" appraisal, for which there will be a charge.

If there are relatives, valuable jewelry should probably stay within the family as heirloom pieces. In fact, even good quality costume jewelry will probably find willing takers within the family.

Inexpensive or "fun" pieces of jewelry would be wonderful gifts for little girls in the family, or young ladies in institutions where they don't get a lot of pretty things, such as homes for the developmentally disabled, mental institutions, orphanages, nursing homes, or perhaps homes for unwed mothers.

Nylon Stockings

Many older women, remembering the unavailability of silk stockings during the Second World War have never been able to bring themselves to dis-

Tout passé
Tout lasse,
Tout casse.

(Everything passes,
Everything wears out,
Everything breaks.)

-French proverb-

pose of those precious old stockings, even though they may be fifty years old and little more than a collection of runners. The good news is that there is still a lot of demand for crocheted or braided rugs made from old nylons. (They wear like iron!) Also, some ingenious crafters have even figured out how to make dolls with quite realistic features out of them. The best way to find the rug ladies or the doll ladies is to call several senior centers or lower income retirement homes.

A thing of beauty is a joy for ever

-From Keats' Endymion-

Personal Hygiene Products

Any organization with female clients can use a continual supply of "lady things." Such places are battered women's shelters, homes for retarded, teen runaway shelters, AIDS hospices, and homeless shelters.

Men's personal care products can be used by men in homeless shelters, boy's homes, low-income residential senior centers, teen runaway shelters, and drug and alcohol rehabilitation centers.

Items they can use are shampoo, conditioner, soap, baby powder, body powder, cloth towels and wash clothes, paper towels, toilet paper, (unopened) deodorant, athlete's foot antifungicidal powder and spray, "jock itch" medications and lice treatments.

Women's Military Uniforms & Memorabilia

A large part of the new Washington, D.C. Women's Memorial commemorating the 400,000 women who volunteered to serve in the U. S. military, consists of their collection of military women's artifacts. They want items both serious and funny, including letters, photos, old uniforms, and gear. In just the first two years, they gathered roughly 55,000 items, including a WWII WAVES issue swimsuit, Spanish American War service papers and photographs, first edition books written by Civil War women, WAC PT uniforms from the 1960s, Desert Storm chemical gear and photos from all eras.

Items they're still looking for include things from World War I; in-country service for both Korea and Vietnam; and the more recent deployments to Grenada, Panama, Desert Shield/Desert Storm; and items from women sent to Rwanda, Somalia, Haiti, Croatia, Bosnia, Afghanistan and Iraq.

They also need items from active duty, National Guard and Reservists as well as service academy women from the 1970's 1980's and 1990s. They particularly need items directly related to assignments, flight suits and gear, for example. Without artifacts, memorabilia, and photographs from all ex-military women, they cannot accurately portray their contributions to the exhibits.

They also want a written synopsis of every ex-service woman's tour of duty. They have a questionnaire they will send out to all who request one.

To donate artifacts, call the Curator's Office at 1-800-222-2294 to discuss the donation. If the donation is accepted, the donor is responsible for shipping or delivery to the foundation.

Their address is:

The Women's Memorial
Dept. 560
Washington, D.C. 20042-0560

P.S. If you're a woman veteran of any branch of the service, be very sure to register with them.

> Women are remarkable! Remember, Ginger Rogers did everything Fred Astaire did, but she did it backwards and in high heels.
> -Faith Whittesey-

How to Dispose of your Stuff

Chapter Ten

MEN'S STUFF

U.S. Military Uniforms and Medals

Old military memorabilia is valuable. Such items as uniforms, medals, unit histories, books, insignias, photos, diaries and patches are in demand and avidly coveted by collectors.

Gear is wanted from all American conflicts. It doesn't matter if it's from Vietnam, Korea, World Wars II or I or even earlier. (In fact, the older it is, the more valuable it is.)

The old uniforms may look quaint and no longer fit but they were worn by handsome brave men who served when duty called.

There are museums of every description, and for every branch of the service. There are battleship museums, battle museums, military medical museums, state military museums, regional military museums, and even museums for relatives of veterans. There's surely a museum or collection that can use whatever military item you have to donate. To find the most appropriate one, do an Internet search using the Google search engine, and search for U.S. Military memorabilia donations or U.S. Military Museums.

Dress uniforms from all branches of the service are also needed by *Bugles Across America*, a patriotic group who believes every veteran whose family wants it, should have a bugler playing a live rendition of "Taps" at the veteran's funeral. Their address is on page 234.

Razors and Shaving Supplies

Men's personal grooming aids can be used by Old Soldiers Homes, missions, homeless shelters, Veterans hospitals, and nursing homes that cater to Alzheimer patients, and fixed income older men who live on their own. Just be sure contents are clearly marked and clean.

Lumber and Building Supplies

A board, 2x4 or piece of plywood is a pretty valuable commodity in this era of skyrocketing lumber prices. Many worthy groups can put new or used lumber to good use, and will be glad to get it.

So what if that pile of good lumber is a few years old? Houses from before the Revolutionary war are still standing and sound.

Habitat for Humanity builds homes for low-income, first-time homebuyers without conventional down payments, by having them put in several hundred hours of work in lieu of money.

Other groups who frequently need various building materials are neighborhood associations, fire departments or church men's groups. They can also use items such as sinks, clean modern toilets, windows and good quality paint.

These good Samaritans take on repair projects for impoverished older people, and do such things as repairing roofs, porches, steps and rotting floors and making plumbing and electrical repairs.

Trade schools that teach building and carpentry can always use wood, as can junior high and high schools with shop classes. (Especially in low income areas where the school district cannot afford to provide such materials.)

Nearly all the above groups will be glad to come pick up the lumber and haul it off.

If you have an old dilapidated barn or ancient falling-down shed, it can be money in the bank. Those old boards can bring in substantial amounts of cash from decorators, architects, cabinetmakers and remodelers. Some use the weathered boards for walls, furniture, antique furniture or floors. Hand-hewn or hand sawn boards and beams are worth their weight in gold, and frequently cost far more than new lumber. So are old recovered river logs. One company that buys such wood is Barn Shadow, 32 Lee Place, Wellsville, NY 14895 (716) 593-5075.

To find a buyer near you, do an Internet search for "barn boards," "reclaimed flooring," "barn siding," or "remanufactured antique wood" or check your Yellow Pages under "Lumber – Used" or "Millwork-Architectural."

Scrap Metal

While little old ladies save mayonnaise jars and old nylons, old men save interesting "parts" to things, and scrap iron. Much to the chagrin of the little old ladies, the old men frequently have yards, garages, sheds and barns full of the stuff! Emptying out the house may be a breeze compared to cleaning out Grandpa's yard, shed and barn.

Again, don't rush to have it hauled off without first finding out what it is. It may actually be valuable (especially parts to old farm equipment or antique cars). There are a number of groups that are aficionados of old vehicles and equipment, and the best battle plan might be to track them down and get a knowledgeable opinion from the experts. Then once you know what you've got, you can confidently call in either the antique dealer or junk man.

Do Not Use at All — Throw Away

Out of what may be thousands of pounds of belongings, there are only a handful of items which cannot be used by others, and should be thrown away, — things such as dentures and old used toothbrushes, some outdated medicines, opened containers of food and items that might be contaminated and things broken or stained beyond repair.

Many well-intentioned people give millions of pounds of totally unusable things to charities, particularly to Thrift Stores. It costs these recipients a fortune to have Dumpsters of the stuff hauled off.

It is better to rust out than to wear out.
-George Whitefield-
(1829-1900)

How to Dispose of your Stuff

Chapter Eleven

TRANSPORTATION & MECHANICAL THINGS

Cars/Trucks/Vehicles

God knows no distance.
-Charleszetta Waddles, Nun-

There are several significant benefits to donating a vehicle to charity: you don't have to hassle with selling a used car: no expensive classified ads to run in the newspaper, no handing strangers your car keys for a test drive, no stressful negotiations with a used-car dealer. You receive a tax deduction for the fair market value of the vehicle. You get to make a sizeable contribution to your favorite charity, and you help the charity further their mission.

The National Kidney Foundation (800) 488-CARS wants used vehicles. Many Senior Service groups, such as Meals on Wheels and food banks will also tow away donated vehicles. So will Search and Rescue Units and Boy Scout troops who take part in rescues. They can use 4-wheel drive and off-road vehicles.

Many vocational technical schools or automotive trade schools also appreciate the donation of used (non-running) vehicles to help train future mechanics in the art of restoring the defunct car or truck.

Union Gospel Missions also want donations of cars, trucks and motor homes, as do Volunteers of America.

On the national scene, the renowned Children's Hospital of Los Angeles welcomes donations of cars, trucks, vans, RVs and boats. Vehicles don't have to be in running condition. To arrange for free pickup, call (800) 380-5257. For donations of other items, call (800) 817-4KIDS.

The way this works may not be as you think. When you call, some sort of used car dealership, not the charity, usually answers the phone. That company comes and gets your car, and then either fixes it or dismantles it for parts, with a portion of the proceeds of the sale going to the charity.

You get a receipt for a donation based on the Blue Book value of the car.

It matters not whether one walks slow or fast through the minefield of life, but rather where he steps.

Determining the Value for Tax Purposes

By law if your vehicle is worth more than $5000, you are required to have it valued by an independent certified appraiser (such as an auto dealer). If the value is less than $5000, you have the right to appraise it yourself.

It's quite easy to determine the fair market value of a car or truck. This can be based on the NADA and Kelly Blue Book pricing. You can also reference local auto sales publications containing ads that reflect the fair market value of your vehicle. If you decide to appraise it yourself, keep a record of how you arrived at its fair market value, and keep a photo of the vehicle.

Most charities receive about 70% of the value of the vehicle. The company that handles the donated vehicle receives about 30% of the value for their services in handling vehicle pickup, transfer and donation paperwork, cleaning and sale of the vehicle, or its parts.

Some organizations sell the vehicles to finance activities of their group. Others are repaired and given to those moving from welfare to work, or families with special needs. Others are used for vocational or auto body training for unemployed people. Monies raised from the sale of these cars pay their tuition.

Once your vehicle is accepted you will be contacted by a towing service to make arrangements for the pick up of it. You need only provide the vehicle, ownership papers (the clear title) and keys.

If you donate a vehicle, be sure to request a receipt from the towing service before you turn over the title and see it go down the street.

And don't forget to cancel your car insurance once you give the car away.

Automotive Supplies

Many Vocational Technical schools or automotive trade schools are also grateful recipients of automotive tools, parts, oil, antifreeze, and the many other items that men stock in their garages.

Used oil and old batteries should be recycled. Many auto parts stores accept used oil for recycling. Batteries contain lead and cannot be disposed of at landfills. They are accepted by battery stores, some Sears stores, and on community recycling days or at community or recycling sites. There are also places listed in the Yellow Pages that accept used batteries, working or not. Some even pay a dollar or two.

To recycle nickel-cadmium batteries, take them to your local electronics, computer equipment or hardware store, or call 1-800-8-BATTERY to find the nearest disposal site.

> Just remember, once you're over the hill you begins to pick up speed.
> -Charles M. Schultz-

Motor Homes, Campers, 5th Wheelers

Because of their size and their value, motor homes, etc. could either be a big problem, or a huge blessing. If it not sold or kept as part of the estate, a motor home could be donated for use as a home for a traveling evangelist or ministry team. It could also be converted to use as a rural county bookmobile, or mobile rural medical or dental clinic.

A motor home could also be used by a civil disaster agency or organization as temporary housing for fire, flood, hurricane or other calamity victims. It could be a temporary on-site office or housing at a far flung outpost or as a combination "command central" - group transport or ambulance for a mountain rescue unit.

If you are a "seasoned" citizen, think twice before doing anything with it. Perhaps it would be perfect to move into yourself. There are many wonderful "senior's only" mobile home parks these days, with every social amenity known to mankind right at hand, and usually with your every need (church, shops, clubs, community center, laundromat, restaurants, classes, etc.) just a few steps away.

Frequently when the snow flies (or shortly before), that's when many such snowbirds head south for the winter. With mobility comes the ability to follow the best of all climes. Since most "Sun-belt" mobile home parks limit stays to two weeks, savvy seniors plan their winters to have clusters of friends stay at the same place at the same time, and then all pick up and move together, and repeat the process at the next place.

A word to the wise regarding selling a recreational vehicle: The best time to sell is spring or early summer when people are anxious to hit the road and thinking about buying an RV. The worst time is after hunting season or vacation season, when there's little need for one until the next summer.

The worst place to sell an RV is in the "Snowbird escape corridor," —Arizona, Florida, New Mexico, etc. The reason is because supply exceeds demand there. Many RV's make one-way trips to the winter sun country, because their owners take ill or expire there, and the vehicle must be put up for quick sale.

The Southwest is a bad place to sell, but a good place to buy. Buyers will have their pick of every make and model on the market, all at extremely competitive prices.

Tires, Rims and Snow Chains

If disposing of the vehicle the wheels, rims or chains belong to, consider including them part of the sale or gift.

If they're "spares", one of the organizations that wants donated cars may take them. An automotive trade school might be able to use them, or try a few calls to one of the groups whose mission includes driving, such as Meals on Wheels, or a group that provides patient rides to doctors and hospitals.

Aircraft

"...They shall mount up with wings like eagles..." (Isaiah 40:31). So shall anyone else you bequeath your aircraft to (should you choose to donate it, instead of sell it, or leave it to a family member or friend.)

Heavier-than-air flying machines are impossible.

-Lord Kelvin- ca. 1895, British mathematician and physicist

There are four primary non-profit groups that use aircraft and aircraft supplies: missionaries, the Civil Air Patrol, groups that fly mercy missions, and search and rescue patrols.

If you happen to have a spare airplane to dispose of, these are the ultimate missionary gift, helping them cut days or weeks of harrowing travel time across jungles, deserts and inhospitable terrain.

For instance, the Nome Chapter of the Christian Pilots Association of Alaska (907) 443-7022, Box 1645, Nome, AK 99762, is looking for a Navajo Chiefton or similar aircraft. The group transports missionaries, pastors and lay workers to the Eskimo villages of northwest Alaska and the Russian Far East.

One of the largest Christian groups is Mission Aviation Fellowship. MAF is a team of aviation and communication specialists who support of more than 300 Christian and humanitarian organizations around the world. Founded in 1945, they operate a fleet of 88 aircraft that reach areas where no other form of transportation can go, transporting food, medical supplies and personnel to deliver the gospel to remote areas. They provide telecommunications services (electronic mail, satellite phones HF radio and other wireless systems) in 22 countries.

> **A boat is a hole in the water into which one pours money.**
>
> **-Old sailor's joke-**

Mission Aviation Fellowship
P.O. Box 3202
Redlands, CA 92373-0998
Phone: (909) 794-1151
Fax: (909) 794-8021
E-Mail: maf-us@maf.org

Boats

Boats and watercraft of all types can be used by kid's camps, Scouts, life saving patrols, search and rescue groups, police and fire marine patrols.

Such groups can also use other water and boat related items, such as life jackets, motors, sails, dinghies, oars, global positioning systems, maps and navigational devices.

Hand Tools and Power Tools

Remember the old adage: "give a man a fish and you feed him for a day, teach a man to fish and you feed him for a lifetime." This is true of tools as well. Give a man tools, teach him to use them, and he can always make a living. Every house needs continual repairs, and a man who can repair things is a man who will always find work.

We heard of one unemployed man who was given a drill. He bought some inexpensive "peep holes" for doors, called himself "Mr. Peepers" and went up and down the street putting peepholes in front doors. By doing several installations per day at $25 each, he was soon making a very nice living.

Tools can be used by halfway houses that rehabilitate drug and alcohol abusers, to equip the residents to go back into the world with a skill and a new direction.

Tools can also be used by any other group that works with men: Scouts, senior centers, Veteran's homes with craft shops, job training programs, and under-funded schools with vocational shops.

The purpose of a father's tools is to teach his son what not to touch until he gets old enough to use them, then he is soon gone from home.

Farm Equipment

Anyone who has traveled through the small towns of America can attest to how many museums and county fairs have collections of old farm equipment. If the machinery and tools you have are in the antique category, check the above, or call your county extension agent for ideas.

If the equipment is still in working order, consider donating it to one of the many live-in drug and alcohol ministries that run farms and ranches to support themselves or groups that farm to grow food for food banks.

This might also be an opportunity to do some one-on-one giving to a worthy young person who wants to become a farmer, or some struggling man who has land and desire, but needs equipment.

Chapter Twelve

YARD & GARDEN ITEMS

House Plants

Many people have plants they have spent many years nurturing, and they want to be assured that their cherished plants will be well cared for and loved, when they become unable to continue doing so themselves.

> That which we call a rose by any other name would smell as sweet
> -Romeo and Juliet-

One woman who knew she was dying had a final get-together for her friends, at which she gave each of them one of her favorite plants. Because of that, memory of her lives on through her plants. "Orissa's plant" is unique to each of them even though they have many other plants, because she comes to mind each time they look at it, water it and enjoy it. If there aren't friends or relatives to give remaining plants to, perhaps a favorite caretaker, store clerk or waitress would enjoy being a recipient. Plants can also be appreciated by giving them to group homes, garden groups, horticulture societies, schools, libraries and churches.

Seeds

If you're one of those meticulous people who have carefully cultivated and maintained a special strain of "heirloom" seeds, (seeds that have remained genetically unaltered for generations), by all means, pass them on to future family gardeners. Those who lovingly tend gardens tell that there's little more satisfying than raising the same plants they remember from their grandparent's gardens. The old unimproved plants may not be as fancy as today's hybrids, but what they lack in "pretty," they more than make up in flavor or sentimentality.

Most "bought" seeds have a shelf life of many years, regardless of the date stamped on the package. Seeds are an especially prized commodity by many missionaries. One group that ships them overseas to countries where they are desperately needed is World Concern Supply Service, (206) 771-5700,

19802 Highway 99, Lynnwood, WA 98036. Postage shouldn't cost much, and not a seed will be wasted. These seeds will be shipped to Third World countries.

Also on the national scene, Widow's Mite Mission (address in appendix under Native American Ministries) loves to get seeds of any kind.

Locally seeds might be appreciated by those who run the local community pea patch, a Future Farmer's of America group, or your County Extension Agent might know of a worthy recipient.

> The creation of a thousand forests is in one acorn.
>
> -Ralph Waldo Emerson-

Shrubs/Trees

Normally trees and shrubs stay with the property, however one idea which should be considered is starting cuttings of especially nice or particularly treasured items. These might include Grandma's favorite rose bush, a distinctive rhododendron, a colorful holly, or say an old apple tree that has been on the property or in the family for many years. A local garden club might appreciate the opportunity to come take cuttings too, since many have plant sales every year, and would relish the opportunity to get some good stock free for the taking.

Lawn Mowers, Yard Tools and Yard Equipment

An enterprising young man needing money for college might be a good recipient. A summer of yard work using your no-longer-needed yard care equipment may give him just the financial start he needs. You'll probably find that person or a young father needing to supplement his income by running a small ad in your local "shopper" paper.

Storage sheds

Garden clubs, community garden plots or low-income "pea-patches" would welcome a storage shed. Call the garden editor of your paper to find the organizers of such projects. Chances are the group will come out, haul if off (dismantling it if necessary) and have it back up in their garden in no time.

Compost Piles, Topsoil, Manure Piles and Worm Bins

Most serious gardeners carefully cultivate their compost piles, taking care to keep them turned, watered and sweet. Nothing would make them happier to know the work of making their precious pile was not for naught. Contribute it to a local garden club, horticulture class or gardener who grows food for the Food Bank. The same is true of manure piles. Manure is only manure if it sits around and becomes aromatic. To a gardener, it's fertilizer, and it's *very* valuable. They'll even come shovel it and happily haul it away.

Many low-income communities have community garden plots or "pea patches" for residents. If situated in the city, they may be trying to grow vegetables in clay or hardpan, and a load of good topsoil, compost, manure or worms would be a welcome addition.

> **One generation plants the trees, another gets the shade**
>
> -Chinese Proverb-

Flower Pots and Planters

Flowerpots seem to have little value, until you need one. Two groups with a continuing need for pots are garden clubs (for their annual plant sales) and high schools that have horticulture classes. You might also check your Yellow Pages and see if your local area or university has an arboretum. They might have some suggestions of who can use them in your area.

Fertilizer, Weed Killer, Garden Chemicals

Unneeded yard and gardening chemicals should be used, whenever possible, rather than recycled. It costs nearly $17 for a recycling facility to recycle a can of weed killer.

Instead give the items to another gardener, a garden club, a young enterprising landscaper, or any facility with grounds to maintain.

Old Gardening Equipment

Don't throw out those old watering cans and quaint wheelbarrows. They may not be any good for gardening anymore, but they may be antiques. For

How to Dispose of your Stuff

Suburbia is where the developer bulldozes out the trees, then names the streets after them.
-Bill Vaughan-

example, painted watering cans can bring $25 to $75 each. Pre-1900 lawn mowers sell for thousands of dollars. Circa 1900 iron lawn gnomes go for $500 each. For more information, check with *Past Times*, (708) 446-0904, Box 1121, Morton Grove, IL 60053.

Chapter Thirteen

FOOD

Food

Food banks can *always* use food. Or you can target your food donations to shelters for abused women, or churches or ministries and organizations that feed the homeless. There aren't many orphanages around these days, but of those that are run by private organizations, most can always use baby food and formula as well as food of any kind.

> When one is hungry, everything tastes good.
> -Unknown-

Another approach for those willing to spend a little time and personal involvement is to pick up any local newspaper and read the daily litany of tragedies, then think for a moment about the victims and survivors. Most stories have many untold underlying misfortunes and unnamed hurting victims.

For instance, a woman we know once read about a man who held up a local gas station, and was shot and killed by a passing Deputy Sheriff. The deceased gunman left a wife and seven children. While in no way condoning what the husband had done, the lady's heart went out to the widow with seven mouths to feed. She cleaned out her cupboards and took several boxes of food to the widow. Upon finding them, she discovered their cupboards were bare and the mother and children hadn't eaten for two days.

"I was hungry and you fed me," still continues to be a worthy admonition.

Another group in desperate need of food is the elderly who subsist only on Social Security. If you know of such a case, you can always be an unheralded angel who leaves a box of food on the doorstep. Many older people raised in the tradition of never accepting "charity" would be too proud to accept it otherwise.

Fresh Food

According to the Department of Agriculture 13.8 billion pounds of perfectly good food wind up in landfills each year.

No one is hurt by doing the right thing.
-old Hawaiian saying-

Should your time to disperse things coincide with harvest time, count your blessings and share the bounty of your garden with others. Although you can't drop 100 zucchinis into the food bank bin, you can take them to the food bank's distribution center. You can also share food with soup kitchens or missions, with people who recently lost a job, are struggling financially, have lots of kids, or are supporting elderly family members, teenagers on their own, or to an institution like a hospice or AIDS house.

Most large cities have groups that will pick up and deliver home grown produce to the food banks. If having a problem finding a local recipient, the Department of Agriculture has a toll-free telephone line - 1-800-GLEAN IT- to help people find out how to rescue more food and find a local distribution network.

If you're lucky enough to live in the citrus belt, and happen to have backyard trees with more oranges than you know what to do with, a common request homeless and runaway kids frequently make, —is for oranges. Apparently they're always in short supply in dumpsters or shelters, wherever the kids go for food. Don't let them rot on the ground when they would be so appreciated by a food bank or shelter.

The Good Samaritan Law

In 1996 Congress passed the Good Samaritan Food Donation Act, which removes liability from anyone who, in good faith, donates food that harms someone, unless there is evidence of gross negligence. Good Samaritan laws are designed to encourage the donation of food and groceries to non-profit charitable agencies by minimizing the liability of donors and distributors of food.

Canned Food and Canning jars

Some gleaner's groups are so meticulous in preventing food waste that they actually "lay up" or can and preserve food that can't be consumed immediately.

Other groups that might appreciate good canning jars would be 4-H kids, Future Farmers young ladies and some church relief societies.

You might also give your local county extension agent a call to see if he/she knows of anyone who might be able to use them.

If you can't feed a hundred people, then feed just one.
-Mother Theresa-

Because of the fear of botulism poisoning, home-canned foods or products made from them are generally not permitted at public events (such as potluck dinners or bazaars). Nor are they accepted as donations to food pantries. But the empty jars are welcome, even if the contents are not.

Vitamins, Dietary Aids and Food Supplements

The diets of many elderly and low-income people are abysmal and lacking in nutrients. If you give food to those groups, you might also tuck in whatever spare vitamins and supplements you have.

Multivitamins (both adults and children's) prenatal vitamins, Vitamin C, B-complex, calcium and iron, can also be used by ministries that ship medicines (page 93) as long as they have a minimum of 18 months left before their expiration date.

Labels, Box Tops and Coupons

Even the packaging that would normally just be thrown in the trash contains major blessings for thousands of young people.

When mailing any of the following items (books of stamps or loose stamps, Campbell Soup labels, Betty Crocker coupons, etc) you can mail them the more economical Third Class rate. Mark the outside of the envelope "Third Class Printed Matter," and be sure to put your name and address in the upper left-hand corner so the group can acknowledge your gift.

Campbell Soup Labels

Imagine! Both delicious fare and school supplies from cans of Campbell's soup.

The great granddaddy of all coupon redemption programs is the "Campbell's Soup Label for Education" effort. Labels can be redeemed for items including computer equipment and software, library materials, playground equipment, child care supplies, food service equipment and even transportation equipment.

For nearly three decades, the Campbell Soup Company has redeemed the front labels of all Campbell's products except Campbell's Ready to Serve soups (save the plastic lids from those) and for Campbell's Dry Soup and Recipe Mix (save the entire box bottom panel with the UPC code from those.)

Other redeemable Campbell's labels are those from the front of Franco American Gravies, SpaghettiO's & Pasta, Pepperidge Farm Breads, Croutons and Cookies, Cakes, Turnovers, Dumplings, Puff Pastry and Phyllo Dough, and Goldfish Crackers and cookies. Also accepted for Campbell's credits are Swanson Broth (paper labels or UPC's from cartons), lids from Pace Salsa Picante, front labels or lids from Prego Pasta sauces and front labels from V8 Vegetable Juice or Splash (or UPC code from 8-packs). These are all Campbell products too.

One worthy group currently working toward saving 1.1 million labels so they can get a minivan, is the Veterans of Foreign Wars National Home for Children. If you have some to donate, mail them to:

VFW National Home for Children
3673 S. Waverly Road
Eaton Rapids, MI 48827

Heinz Baby Food Labels

If you happen to have a collection of Heinz Baby Food labels to donate, you can help hospitalized kids' parents with uncovered medical expenses. Heinz donates six cents for each label Akron's Children's Hospital collects. Send your labels (fronts of labels only) to:

Children's Hospital Volunteer Department
One Perkins Square
Akron, OH 44308-1062

General Mills Box Top$ 4 Education

General Mills "Box Top$ 4 Education" helps students earn cash for the things their school really needs. It pays up to $10,000 to pay for school programs, materials, supplies or equipment, which really comes in handy these days with rising costs and shrinking school budgets.

This simple idea has become a successful fundraiser for more than 60,000 enrolled K-8 schools nationwide. Parents, students and schools have earned over $50 million in donations from General Mills since 1996.

The cereal is just one part of the package. The box tops are equally valuable.

Save the "Box Tops 4 Education" coupon from over 330 participating General Mills products, and turn them into cash for your favorite school. (Other General Mills products accepted are Yoplait ® Yogurt, Betty Crocker ® products and Lloyds ® Barbeque products.)

If your local schools aren't collecting General Mills Box Top$ 4 Education, St. Judes Ranch for Children (page 149) (800) 492-3562, would love to have them.

Trading Stamps

Remember those wonderful little stamps that could be redeemed for everything from a coffee pot to a mink coat? Trading stamps, (such as S&H Green Stamps, Gold Bond, Blue Chip and Orange Stamps) were immensely popular in the 60's and 70's, but many are now relics of the past. Not all, however, in some areas (primarily in the south) you can still earn stamps at some grocery stores.

Trading stamps never lose their value if the company that issued them is still around. Green Stamps are now called "green points." You can redeem the stamps or points or see what they can be redeemed for, by logging on to their website at (www.greenpoints.com). For Blue Chip stamps you have to call an 800 number to request a catalog and then send in the stamps to get your selection. To redeem Blue Chips, call (800) 824-0655.

If you want to donate stamps, S&H Green Stamps, Gold Bond and Blue Chip stamps can be put to good use by Widow's Mite Mission (page 206).

Another group who would like them is the Tamassee DAR School, a school for the mountain children of poverty, abuse, neglect or misunderstanding run by the Daughters of the American Revolution, (864) 944-1390.

The Tamassee DAR School
P.O. Box 8
Tamassee, SC 29686-0008

They collect S&H Green stamps, Top Value stamps, Plaid stamps, Greenbox stamps and Blue Chip stamps. They also collect Campbell Soup labels.

The Crossnore School, a North Carolina home for disadvantaged children, also needs top Value, S&H Green Stamps, Gold Stamps and Plaid Stamps.

Crossnore School
P.O. Box 249
Crossnore, NC 28616
(704) 733-4305

Freebie Coupons

Such a simple thing a label or coupon is, but oh how much good they can do!

Many businesses reward repeat business customers every so often with a free item for every so many purchased. If you have some unneeded unredeemed cards for haircuts, pizza, Subway ® sandwiches, or other items, consider donating them to the Salvation Army. They always know of worthy recipients.

Chapter Fourteen

Medicines and Medical Aids

Medicines

We take having good medicines for granted and forget there are millions of others in this world who have never had so much as an aspirin. Most drugs (not all) have years of shelf life beyond the expiration date marked on their containers, and while they cannot be sold in the United States, they can still be shipped overseas. It is "expired" or outdated drugs and medicine samples that make up the only medicines many medical missionaries have to dispense.

There are millions of people in this world who have never had so much as an aspirin.

Ministries that repackage bulk medicines for shipment overseas have to be licensed by the Food and Drug Administration. All have registered pharmacists on staff, who know which medications are still safe to use, and which deteriorate with age. There aren't many of these "medicine ministries" around any more. This means that if you have medicines you'd like to donate, you'll probably have to ship them (prepaid shipping) to one of the ministries. Call first to make sure they can use what it is you have to donate.

You might also check with your church or denomination office for the name of medical missionaries they support and ask how supplies are shipped to them.

Some local organizations can use generic medicines, however most aren't allowed to dispense even so much as a cold pill. For instance, a state Old Soldier's home can dispense medicine, but a homeless shelter probably cannot. The difference lies in whether or not they have a medical staff.

Medicines that ministries (like World Concern) can still accept are: antacids (Rolaids®, Mylanta ®), anti-diarrheal medications, antibiotics (adult and pediatric - oral and perenteral), antihistamines, aspirin, acetaminophen and ibuprofen, cold remedies, eye and ear ointments, pediatric medications, skin ointments (steroid, antibiotic, antifungal), Pedialyte, asthmas medications and bronochodilators. Keep in mind these must be new, unopened, and have at least 18 months left before their expiration date.

Small Medical Supplies

In this country, disposable latex gloves cost mere pennies a pair and are strictly intended for one-time use, but in Third World countries, they're a precious commodity that gets used again and again. U.S. hospitals discard $200 million worth of recyclable supplies annually, according to researchers at the Yale University School of Medicine.

General medical supplies needed are: Ace bandages, alcohol and Betadine wipes, Band-Aids, gauze dressings (all types), gloves (sterile and non-sterile), prep trays, scrub solutions, spinal trays, surgical masks, suture (absorbable non-absorbable and silk), suture sets, syringes (all sizes with needles) tape (all types) and wound care trays.

Medicine left in the bottle can't help heal the sick. -Yoruba saying-

Diagnostic supplies are laryngoscopes, otoscopes and ophthalmoscopes, portable ultrasounds, specula (ear and nasal), sphygmomanometers, stethoscopes and fetoscopes, thermometers, tongue depressors and vagilal specula.

Instruments needed included: forceps, hemostats (straight, curved and mosquito), needle holders, retractors, scalpel handles and blades, and scissors (surgical and bandage).

IV supplies include arm boards, butterfly IV's (any size), intracaths (18g or smaller), IV administration sets and IV prep trays.

Laboratory supplies are cell counters, centrifuges, microscopes, pipettes, slide covers, slides, sterilizers and urine test strips.

Always needed are such orthopedic supplies as casting material, crutches, limb braces and supports, and splints.

Patient care items are gowns, lotion, shampoo, soap (wrapped) toothbrushes and toothpaste.

Pediatric supplies needed are blood pressure cuffs, disposable diapers, feeding tubes and scalp vein needles.

Ministries that can use these supplies are:

World Concern
19802 Highway 99
Lynnwood, WA 98036
(425) 771-5700,

Northwest Medical Teams, Intl
(contact: Dan Hudson)
6955 SW Sandburg Street
Portland, OR 97223
(503) 624-1000, fax: (503) 624-1001
email: nwmti@transport.com

This group has a variety of projects that involves sending medical teams worldwide. They have gone to Romania since 1989 and operate a clinic in Mexico. They also dig wells so children aren't dying from unclean water.

> Our outdated medical equipment is state of the art to Third World doctors who have none.

Large Medical Supplies and Equipment

Many mission hospitals operate with antiquated and broken down equipment, so the last thing we want to do is ship them more of the same. But if you have any good quality, fully-functioning medical equipment to donate, call World Medical Mission at (828) 363-1980 and talk to a bio-medical technician.

Mechanical tables and equipment are preferred over equipment that is dependent upon electricity to operate. Equipment that requires electricity should function on both 50 and 60 HZ or be easily convertible to different voltages and frequencies.

Since most medical equipment requires various accessories to function properly, please make every effort to find all the accessories and manuals that go with it, including patient cables and transducers, power cords, recorder paper, spare parts and operator and service manuals.

They can also use medical textbooks published within the last five years.

Mercy Ships International can also use large and some small medical supplies. Call them at (903) 939-7000 to find their current needs. They are also listed on page 232.

Old Hearing Aids

Hear Now is a national, non-profit organization that recycles used hearing aids and distributes them to deaf and hard-of-hearing persons with limited financial resources. Ship the old hearing aid in a small box or padded envelope with your complete mailing address to:

Hear Now
9745 East Hampden Ave., Suite #300
Denver, CO 80231-4923
For further information call: 1-800-648-4327

Old Eye Glasses

He that is stricken blind cannot forget the precious treasure of his eyesight lost.
-Wm. Shakespeare-

The gift of sight remains within a pair of eyeglasses. Old eyeglasses could be as precious as gold to those in need of them. Volunteer Optometrists for Service to Humanity (VOSH) is an organization of optometrists who collect old eyeglasses and match them to needy people in developing countries. VOSH members travel to the countries and donate their time and professional skills to run optical tests and fit participants with eyeglasses that match their prescriptions. In 1991, over 9,000 people in Ecuador alone were given the gift of better sight through the efforts of VOSH and all those who donated old eyeglasses.

Most opticians and optometrists also accept used lenses and frames for reuse, as do Lions Clubs all over the country. LensCrafters stores collect glasses for Lion's Clubs. Call 800-74 SIGHT to find the location closest to you. These glasses are refurbished, classified by prescription and distributed to people in developing countries through ministries such as Mercy Ships International.

Another group that collects old eyeglasses is Habitat for Humanity's "Vision Habitat" program. They collect old eyeglasses (including near and far-sighted glasses, bifocals and sunglasses). They run them through a "lensometer" which "reads" the glasses' prescription and prints it out onto a cash register-type receipt, which is then stapled around the bow of the glasses. The glasses are then sold for $1 to $2 a pair overseas.

A 55 gallon drum holds about 800 pair of glasses, making each barrel worth about $1,600, the approximate cost of a house overseas. All money raised from the sale of used eyeglasses stays in the country where the glasses are sold. Since 1985, Vision Habitat has built over 130 houses overseas from the sale of glasses. Contact:

> Vision Habitat
> c/o Habitat for Humanity International
> 121 Habitat Street
> Americus, GA 31709-3498.
> (912) 924-6935

Mobility and Geriatric Aids

Orthopedic devices, wheelchairs (both manual and electric)), walkers, adult potty chairs, toilet safety frames, hospital beds, crutches and canes can always be used by nursing homes, senior centers and fire departments. They can also be a Godsend to many MS patients and to seniors struggling to survive on an inadequate, fixed income.

To find someone who needs what you have, call your local MS Society, senior center (they usually have a community coordinator who knows local seniors and their needs), or your local visiting nurse service. Many churches are also aware of needy seniors or can use the items as loaners. Put the word out about what you have, and you'll soon wish you had several similar items to give away.

He who limps is still walking.
-Stanislaw J. Lec-

Most local fire departments welcome donations of used wheel chairs too. They keep them as loaners for local people in need or for when local people have guests who may need a wheelchair short term, but couldn't bring their own.

How to Dispose of your Stuff

Chapter Fifteen

PAPERS, PAPERS, PAPERS

Your "Body of Work"

This is a special category, which to many people is the most important of all. The summation of what you do or have done for a living, plus many of your hobbies and interests, is probably reduced to an accumulation of paper that can be stored in anything from a shoebox to rooms of files. Thus, many people's files represent their life's work.

Such things could be scientific papers, scholarly findings, and files resulting from a lifetime of research, or creative endeavors such as musical scores, writings or poetry. They might be works in progress. They might also be artistic works, such as sketches and art projects and dance diagrams. Teachers usually have collections of teaching aids.

Unfortunately these papers are frequently looked upon as worthless by many inheriting the task of sorting someone else's belongings. But be assured there are MANY people, groups, libraries and institutions that would be interested in such papers, whatever the subject.

Blessed is the person who pays scrupulous care and attention to the disposal of another's files!

Bury my body in the ground and my memory in history, but bury not my works in eternity, for I wish them to live forever, for it is those that I am.
-Unknown-

Personal Papers, Clipping Files and Ephemera

If you are fortunate enough to still be alive to do your own planning, start *now* to arrange for the disposition of your papers and files, then leave copious notes and directions! If your files, writings and clippings are particularly dear to your heart and you want them to "live on," than practice the old admonition, "do your giving while you're living, then you're knowing where it's going."

Who is a soul mate that would most appreciate the contents of your files? A friend? A professional colleague? A fellow amateur researcher? An author who writes on your subject or area of expertise? An organization? A library? Maybe even an adversary! How about a protégé, a young person with an interest in your area of knowledge or interest?

A lighthouse is a waste of time, money and energy until it is needed.

Perhaps your files should be divided and go to several different places, depending on subject and contents.

Ideas for who might want files are:

o State historical societies/libraries/museums

o County historical societies/libraries/museums

o Local historical societies/libraries/museums

o Private historical societies/libraries/museums

o Trade Associations

o Professional organizations (national/state/local)

o University libraries

o Corporate or company libraries

o A local trade school, community college or high school

o Another researcher who shared the same love of your favorite topics you did.

o A student who showed an interest in your research

The beauty of giving your papers to one of the above is many fold. Not only will your files and collections "live on," they will be accessible to benefit many others, and best of all you will still have full access to and use of them yourself, you just won't have to store them!

If you choose to keep your papers and have them dispersed later, to really help whoever may have to dispose of them, tag or mark each file folder as to eventual recipient. This could be done one of several ways, but the safest way is to write the name of the intended recipient on the front of each file folder.

Makes notes such as "Knox County Library," or your local historical society. The new recipient can always put them in new file folders.

Sticky notes inside or outside each file folder are not really a good option, since they fall off easily.

Giving Copyrights, Trademarks, Intellectual Property, etc.

To donate rights to your published works such as writings, books, logos, art, photographs, or music, you must convey the copyright rights in writing, clearly spelling out that the copyright ownership of the work is being transferred to the charity. The transfer must be signed by the creator/owner of the rights conveyed or his or her authorized agent. This is as per 17 U.S.C. Section 201 (b). The transfer of the work and its copyright is considered a charitable contribution and is usually tax-deductible if addressed to a qualified donee.

You cannot live without lawyers, and you certainly cannot die without them.
-Joseph Choate-

The charity will give you an "Acknowledgment of Donation" form that acknowledges and accepts the generous gift.

It is best to consult your attorney if there are royalties or income involved. Your heirs might wish to have the asset stay in the family, so consider that option too if the work is particularly valuable.

Books

While most large metropolitan libraries bulge with vast book collections, many rural towns and counties have very limited library collections. Pick out the smallest or poorest county around, and ask if they would be interested in what books and collections you have. Who knows? Some small, hungry mind may be inspired and challenged by your old books, and grow up to be the next Einstein or Bill Gates.

Many prisons also have libraries, and if your books are of the variety to help people "straighten up and fly right," this might be a good home for them. Other good homes for books might be county or city jails, adult literacy programs, homeless shelters and women's shelters.

Local home-school groups frequently maintain their own lending libraries. Some of your books may be of value to them, especially if you were a teacher or have educational books.

You never know what the gift of those books may lead to. When John Harvard (1607-1638), a young minister and teacher, left half of his estate and his entire library, all 320 volumes, to a proposed college he wanted to help, he bequeathed what he treasured most.

Although not a huge financial bequest, Harvard's gift "brought in the intellectual influences and opened the intellectual resources which gave the College a better life than any material possessions could give." Oh yes, and because of his gift of books, they named the college after him. You may have heard of it, - Harvard University.

In a section or two you will read about another group, *Bridge to Asia*, which sends literature to Asia. They need dictionaries, encyclopedias, almanacs, atlases, glossaries, thesauruses, test-preparation books, and college, graduate and professional texts. Their address is listed following the "National Geographics" section on page 105.

Groups who help resettle immigrants and refugees can always use english dictionaries.

If you want to sell books, magazines, record albums, CDs, cassettes, computer programs or videos, Half Price Books (the national chain) will make you an offer on just about anything printed or recorded that comes its way. Don't expect to get much though, because they guy cheap and sell cheap.

Christian Books

Christian books are paper missionaries! Though they may be old and the paper yellowed, the pages of most still contain the way to Eternal Life, according to the followers of the faith.

Today a reader, tomorrow a leader.
-W. Fusselman-

Choices for disposal of these collections range from giving them to a pastor for his personal library and for his dispersal, or giving them to a Christian school, to shipping them overseas to a country hungering for Christian literature.

Prisons ministries would also be ideal recipients. Check with your nearest chapter of Full Gospel Businessmen International to see if they can use what you have in their prison ministry.

You might also list the looks or library on the Christian church on-line swap meet (at www.rca.org/resource/swapread.html) This is a ministry of the Reformed Church in America, but it serves churches and Christian organizations of all sizes and denominations.

Christian Books are paper missionaries, traveling the world with their Good News.

Bibles other than the Family Bible

While millions of people around the world will live and die without ever seeing a Bible, most American homes have at least one, if not several lying around.

Many good overseas ministries have a never-ending need for all the Bibles they can get. Bibles, even after the death of the owner, can still continue to spread the Good News, and bring more souls into the kingdom.

Some ministries that can use bibles are listed on page 210.

If you happen to have a particularly rare, old or valuable Bible you wish to donate to a museum, you might consider contacting:

The International Book and Bible Museum
215 NW 10th
Oklahoma, OK 73103
(405) 235-5145

Christian Tracts

Tracts (especially Chick Tracts) and Gospels of John can be taken into prisons, and one ministry that can use them is Bible Believers Fellowship. They can also use New Testaments and bibles. Many prisons do not allow hard cover books, therefore the materials should all be of the soft cover type, and they can use them in both English and Spanish.

> Bible Believers Fellowship, Inc.
> P.O. Box 0065
> Baldwin, NY 11510-0065

Professional Records, Papers and Files

Yes, there are many folks who have other people's papers in their possession. Doctors, dentists, lawyers and accountants all are required to maintain records of patients and clients. What happens to those records upon the death of the holder?

There is no standard length of time such records must be maintained, because each state sets its own rules. In one state a doctor's patient files may be disposed of after 3 years, while in another state they must be kept available for 7 years.

Who must they be available to? Other doctors, lawyers and (possibly) accountants, and/or the patients or clients themselves who might need them. Insurance companies, IRS or other branches of government (such as Workmen's comp), police departments, or the courts may also frequently demand them. If they're in your care, you must be able to produce them. If there are VOLUMES of files, it might be wise to rent a storage unit, rather than give up your garage or a bedroom or two to storage.

If you are responsible for the professional papers, do not destroy any such records until you check your state regulations to see how long the files must be kept. Because of the privacy issue involved, when the time comes that they finally can be destroyed, you may be required to hire a professional disposal company to shred or burn them. If that is what your state law requires, be sure to keep the disposal receipt so you can prove it was done lawfully if you're ever challenged.

Newspapers

Many people have newspaper collections that are/were of immense importance to themselves, but are of little value to those who inherit the job of dis-

> The unrecorded past is none other than our old friend, the tree in the primeval forest which fell without being heard.
> -Barbara Tuchman-
> NY Times, March 8, 1964

posing of them. The first rule of thumb is don't haul them off to the dump. If you're hauling them at all, make it to a recycling center. Newsprint prices vary, but recent prices have been as high as $200 per ton.

But before disposing of them in any manner, take time to see exactly what they are, how old they are, and whether they might have even more value as collectibles. First see if there are any visible notes or clues as to why they were kept. Perhaps they contain a special letter to the editor or article the deceased had penned.

> Newspapers are dead trees with history smeared on them.
> -Horizon, Electronic Frontier-

If the papers are particularly old, sort them into piles according to whether they are "Big Dailies", county papers, local papers or newsletters. Then call the various newspapers and see if they need them for *their* own collections. (All newspapers keep "morgues" and copies of all past editions.) Next call the town library and see if they could use them. Then move on to the county library, and state library. If you still can't find a taker, try the state, county and local historical societies. Finally, check with the genealogy societies. If the papers are old enough, they might have someone who would take on the project of reading them all in hopes of gleaning some gems regarding their area of interest.

Preposterous as it may sound, the government may even be interested in them if they're really old. The National Endowment for the Humanities is the division handling the U.S. Newspaper Project, the Herculean task of microfilming old newspapers. Contact them through the Preservation Office at (202) 707-5213.

One antique collector recently purchased the entire contents of a bedroom at a Seattle estate sale for $1,000, and when going through it, found a box of old comic books buried under a stack of newspapers and magazines. He eventually sold the comics for $60,000.

Finally after all these resources are exhausted, then think of recycling. The next question is who will get the money from selling them to the recycler? (They sell for about a penny to a cent and a half per pound.) After carrying a few loads of heavy papers from the house to your car, you may decide you'd gladly let a charity have the proceeds in exchange for doing the work of hauling them off. (Tip: Newspapers are weighty and clumsy to carry. It makes the job easier if you pack them in brown paper grocery bags and carry them out in a wagon, cart or hand truck.)

Newsletters

Newsletters are mini-gold mines, both from historical and genealogical interest (and frequently other reasons as well.) Since newsletters are usually local in nature, the name and information by and about the deceased is more likely to be found in a newsletter than in a newspaper. Thus even if the newsletters are not of interest to you or your family, others who might be named in the publication may treasure them.

Also, if the organization that published the newsletter is still in existence, it might be happy to find there's a treasure trove of their old newsletters.

Many university libraries also have vast collections of newsletters. It would be worth a phone call to see if they are interested in what you've got.

National Geographics Magazines

There is more treasure in books than in all the pirate's loot on Treasure Island, and best of all, you can enjoy these riches every day of your life. -Walt Disney-

Don't throw out those shelves and shelves of yellow gold, they're real treasures in more way than one. One group, "Bridge to Asia" can't get enough copies of National Geographics. They ship them to China, Vietnam, and Cambodia where 1,000 universities need material in all subjects. Knowledge-starved people line up before dawn to get into libraries the minute they open. Old copies of National Geographics give them a window to the world that few have ever dreamed existed. (In China alone, 250 million adults use English, and students learn our language in early grades.)

In Vietnam, dozens of universities need complete libraries, and thousands of high schools need textbooks and readers.

The National Library of Cambodia and Phnom Penh University need basic texts and references; village schools need readers, vocational-technical manuals, picture books and magazines of all kinds.

To ship your old copies, box them up and ship them U. S. Mail "Library Rate" (about $15.00 for a 60 lb. Box) to San Francisco. They cannot reimburse for shipping or mailing costs, however out-of-pocket expenses are tax deductible together with the value of the publications. (*Library rate may be used to, from, or between a nonprofit organization, and an individual who has no financial interest in the sale, promotion, or distribution of the materials. If your post office challenges you, tell them this is as per "Standard Mail B, Library Mail – 653 – Quick Service Guide.) Bridge To Asia is a 501 (c) (3) non-profit organization.

Ship books (or deliver if you live in the San Francisco area) to:

Bridge to Asia
Osgood Warehouse Services
Pier 23
San Francisco, CA 94111

To contact Bridge to Asia, their office is at:

450 Mission Street, Suite 407
San Francisco, CA 94105
(415) 356-9043
E-mail: asianet@bridge.org

National Geographics magazines are worth money too. One friend's donation of old National Geographics to her favorite foundation netted the group $290. One bookstore paid $40 for some of the magazines, and another store paid $250 for the balance

The colorful magazines also have plenty of willing takers among teachers, home-schoolers, public schools, libraries, senior centers, and various institutions.

National Geographics is America's most collected magazine for good reason.

> Any book that helps a child to form a habit of reading, to make reading one of his deep and continuing needs, is good for him.
> -Richard McKenna-

Readers Digest Condensed Books

We must admit, finding a home for these books almost stumped us! We spent many hours searching the Internet to see who would welcome these wonderful tomes. Time and again, up came places that wanted books, amended by "but please, NO Readers Digest Condensed Books."

Then suddenly we struck gold! A program called The Book Project, operated (surprisingly) by the World Bank! Several times a year, World Bank ships 20-foot containers containing approximately 20,000 books to developing countries. Once at their destination, the books are distributed by the various Ministries of Education, the Peace Corps, Rotary International, The Kenya Girl Scout Association, World Bank staff and spouses, as well as local library boards and local book foundations.

In addition to Readers Digests and Readers Digest Condensed Books, they want textbooks (elementary to senior level – all subjects), ESL books, Discovery Magazine, adult and children's stories for all ages, teacher training aids, college books suitable for continuing education, vocational (crafts) books, French textbooks and stories for native speakers. They can also use encyclopedia and other reference books no older than 15 years, and National Geographic magazines.

Before shipping books, call them at (202) 473-8960. Once you get the go-ahead, ship the books to:

The Book Project
c/o The World Bank Loading Dock
1775 G Street NW
Washington, DC 20433

If you're going to deliver them, call the loading dock to be sure they'll be there to receive deliveries. The loading dock phone number is (202) 473-5363.

Closer to home, some nursing homes welcome Readers Digest Condensed Books too.

> When the pupil is ready, the teacher will come.
> -Chinese proverb-

Encyclopedias and Text Books

One wag observed that there's nothing more obsolete than an old encyclopedia unless it's an ancient textbook. They suggested using them as door-stops.

Fortunately, most deserve a better fate. Unless they truly are ancient, a little detective work should find a recipient for them. Many inner city children have never seen an encyclopedia, much less owned one. The same goes for refugee families who may find reading them useful in helping to learn English.

If they are less than 15 years old, Bridge to Asia or the Book Project may take them.

Other Magazines

Magazines may be old and dated, but their colorful pictures are often enjoyed and treasured by children and residents of homes for the retarded and many in senior centers.

Many back issues or no longer published local or specialty magazines might be wanted by local libraries, schools, historical societies and museums. Once magazines reach 40-50 years of age, they turn into collectibles, and frequently bring substantial sums.

One group that can always use lots of magazines is the USO lounge at most metropolitan airports. (Yes, that is not a misprint. There are still such lounges at most large airports for traveling military personnel and their families.) The lounges can also always use gifts of tea, coffee, snacks, and toys as well.

Doctors' and dentist offices and hospital waiting lounges also go through great quantities of magazines, although most only want current issues. Barber and beauty shops can always use magazines, as can some carryout restaurants where you have to wait while food is prepared. Just be sure to remove your mailing label.

Another group of appreciative recipients are our servicemen and women serving overseas. Find a parent of a young serviceman and they can ship them

Reading makes immigrants of us all. It takes us away from home, but more important, it finds homes for us everywhere.
-Hazel Rochman-

at reasonable rates to an APO stateside at a reasonable cost. The GI's are grateful for American reading material.

Many libraries also put out piles of "freebies" (outdated magazines) for patrons to take, and they might just let you add yours to the collection. Some sell the old literature for a nickel or dime per publication, in which case your cast-off magazines would bring a small contribution to the local library fund.

In addition to National Geographic magazines, Bridge to Asia, also needs journals, magazines, maps, syllabuses, lecture notes, newsletters, teaching aids, sheet music, audiotapes, CD-ROMS and other forms of information. (Examples of journals and magazines they can use are American Scholar, Atlantic, Economist, Foreign Affairs, Harpers, Hudson Review, Mother Jones, The Nation, Nature, New Yorker, Poetry, Reader's Digest, Science, Smithsonian, Utne Reader, Wilson Quarterly, Yale Review.)

They can NOT use American history textbooks, computer books keyed to specific systems, foreign language books (other than English), 'life-style' books, personal development, cookbooks, or pet care, New Age, and books that proselytize a religion or political view.

Those who might want to sell their collectible magazines might want to check on the Internet at (www.trussel.com/books/magdeal.htm) for a list of 76 dealers who buy old magazines, periodicals and ephemera and resell them on the Internet. Some also buy old sports programs.

One such dealer is George Kaufer, Collectible Magazines, 4104 East 14th Street, Vancouver, WA 98661. (800) 896-6751. Email: Gkaufer@aol.com. He currently has over 30,000 different magazines in stock and is in the market to buy more.

Old telephone books are treasures. They document who lived where and when.

Telephone Books

Most libraries now have the entire nation's phone numbers on microfiche or CD-ROM, and no longer have to store the entire phone books. Phone books are best disposed of by contributing them to the annual Kiwanis Phone Book Drive or whoever recycles them in your neighborhood.

This single recycling effort really pays. Qwest Dex estimates over 2.5 million trees, 1 billion gallons of water, 529,872 barrels of oil and more than 620 million kilowatt hours of energy have been saved by people who recycle their phone books through the Qwest Dex recycling effort.

Really old telephone books may be wanted by your county library or genealogy society.

Cardboard

Cardboard is sort of the "pig's squeal" of disposables. You can use virtually every part of the pig but the squeal. When you get rid of everything else, you'll still have a lot of cardboard and boxes. Many recycling centers today are run by groups trying to provide employment for the handicapped and retarded. Donating the cardboard to these worthy groups pays big dividends to the laborers in meaningful productivity, self-esteem because of holding a job, and the joy of earning a paycheck, not to mention helping to save a few trees.

Stop and wonder, - how beautiful was the tree that gave its all to make this cardboard?

If you sell cardboard to a commercial recycler, it brings about $100 per ton (5 cents per pound).

General cardboard recycling rules are that cardboard boxes must be flattened. Wax coated boxes cannot be recycled. Plastic or wax paper wrapping or liners (such as the bags inside cereal boxes) must be discarded. Some home collection recyclers want it set out in a special way (bundled, tied, etc.

Chapter Sixteen

HOUSEHOLD GOODS

Furniture

Since it costs money to move furniture, the closer to home you can dispose of it, the better. Many people need furniture: immigrants and refugees, newlyweds, new parents, battered wives, single parents, not to mention schools, shelters and camps. There is virtually nothing that people aren't glad to get. Especially prized are couches, dressers, shelves, tables, chairs, beds and lamps.

Even the ugliest old chair looks beautiful as it pulls away in someone else's van.

There are many organizations in the resettlement business that always need furniture and lots of it. These are organizations that help people who have lost everything in fires, floods tornadoes or hurricanes. Other groups always needing furniture are refugee resettlement services. They provide temporary housing to newly arriving immigrants and help set them up in housekeeping.

Such groups are: World Relief and Jewish Family Service. Both are described on page 230.

Lamps

Few homes or institutions have too many lamps. The most worthy recipient might be some young person. In many lower income homes, there isn't enough income to provide lamps for each child to do homework by, and a lifetime of poor eyesight can begin by straining to work or read under poor lighting conditions. If you don't know of such a young person, you might call your local school and ask the school counselor if they might know of some worthy recipient.

Check the cord and socket to be sure they're in good condition before donating them. If they show wear, tear or damage, or are old and cracked and hard, do not give them away because they may be a fire hazard or expose someone to electrical shock.

Mattresses and Bedding

Many places and groups can use bedding (sheets, blankets and pillows) but mattresses are harder to dispose of. Many charities that can use them take them on the condition that they are delivered. Groups that always need mattresses are the above-mentioned refugee resettlement groups, such as World Relief or the Jewish Refugee Services.

My bed will comfort me, my couch will ease my complaint.
-Job 7:13

The flood of incoming refugees has slowed considerably from a few years ago when several hundred thousand Vietnamese, Russian and Ukrainian refugees landed on our shores. After a brief time with sponsors, most struck out to set up housekeeping and pursue the Great American Dream. Most were grateful for any furnishings that help them get started. People who have never slept on anything but a grass mat or a mud or wooden floor look upon many mattresses that are unacceptable by our standards as luxuries.

If you can't find a taker for mattresses, you can always call one of the conventional charities that run thrift shops. They usually have their own workshops to rebuild mattresses, and they will pick them up. Another way is to run a freebie ad in a local neighborhood newspaper. There are always families who can use another mattress.

Even old blankets with tears and holes are coveted by quilters who repair them and use them for the inner layer of new quilts. To find recipients, check with churches that might have older congregations and quilting societies. These dedicated ladies haunt rummage sales and thrift stores looking for just such blankets to give them another lease on life.

Your old blanket may end up half way around the globe as a treasured possession that warms a new mother or ailing old person.

Drapes, Blinds and Window, Shades

Start by checking with state institutions that house people, such as homes for the retarded and old soldiers' homes. Since such facilities tend to be placed

at the tail end of government budgets, such ameni-
ties as window dressings probably aren't very high
priority. Drapes, blinds and shades don't seem like
items of great importance, except to the person with
no privacy, or for relief from a cold draft or beating
sun. Start with institutions, group homes, the elderly,
and low-income housing.

People who live in glass houses, should use drapes, shades or blinds.

Rugs and Carpets

Wall-to-wall carpets generally stay with
the house, although occasionally people take it up
to expose a hardwood floor underneath, or because
it's the wrong color or some other aesthetic reason.

Good carpeting and/or rugs can frequently be
used by group homes, schools, newlyweds, immigrants, refugees, private schools or pre-schools, college dorms, college students, people who have suffered a calamity, and seniors on fixed incomes.

Wall Décor

Group homes and institutions that should be
brightened up a little can frequently use pictures,
paintings, mirrors, wall hangings, photos, sconces and
other items of wall décor. Certain wall items might
be appropriate to donate to your (free) community
health center, since those places are frequently sterile and drab, and would benefit from a little cheery
color too.

Wallpaper

If there's a sufficient quantity to paper a room or
more, check with organizations that run live-in cottages or homes, such as teen runaway havens, hospices, halfway homes, women's shelters, adult day
care centers and retirement homes.

If you want to help someone learn a trade, donate the paper to a vocational school with home
remodeling and maintenance courses.

Wallpaper serves many purposes besides covering walls. It's a valuable commodity with childcare
providers, who use it for craft projects.

Fire Extinguishers and Smoke detectors

Smoke detectors:
Don't leave a
home without one.

These items will have universal appeal. Just about any organization could use more of each, however some elderly low-income person who probably has no fire warning or suppression equipment might best use them. Check with your local senior center to see if they have a senior advocate who might know of a needy recipient.

One word of caution. Don't donate an older smoke detector which may malfunction. An antiquated non-working unit is worse than no unit at all because just having one could lull people into a false sense of security. Since even the best new 10-year guarantee detectors cost only about five dollars, if you find someone who really needs one, be a Good Samaritan and just buy them one (plus a battery).

Household Chemicals

Most homes and garages would yield several boxes of chemicals, - soaps and detergents, drain openers, cleansers, oven cleaner, bug killers, and various sprays and powders. The space under most sinks looks like our own private little hazardous waste dump.

These items are expensive to buy, but even more expensive to dispose of if you take them to a recycling center. It costs $13 to dispose of a gallon of toilet bowl or oven cleaner, for instance. It's far better to put the stuff to its intended use.

Many charitable groups are willing to take even partial containers of household chemicals provided they're well marked as to contents. Shipping them would create more problems than you want to deal with, so give them to a local group home, church or charity who is willing to take them. Be careful they don't go someplace where children could get into them.

Fuel (Gas, Oil, Propane and Firewood)

Each year a few tragic stories turn up in the paper about some poor old soul who froze to death in his/her apartment. If you have fuel to dispose of, check with your Visiting Nurse Service and see if these folks know of any needy older people. Salvation Army also has a winter heat program for the needy, although they usually want money instead of the actual fuel.

Any kind of fuel is a valuable commodity to someone who is cold.

Some Christian fuel oil and propane gas companies will even come and pump it out of your tanks and deliver these contributions to the needy at no charge. To find one who will, start by looking in the Yellow Pages and look for those dealers displaying the Christian fish symbol in their ads.

If you are selling your home and intend to pump out the fuel oil and contribute it, be sure to note in your listing agreement that the fuel will be removed and the tank will be nearly empty.

Chapter Seventeen

KITCHEN EQUIPMENT

Appliances - large and small

Camps serve thousands of meals per week during the summer, but soup kitchens and shelters serve them year- round. Most have not one, but several large stoves and refrigerators, and can frequently use another one.

Other useful contributions might be stove hoods, vents, venting systems, big tables, benches, and cabinets. That's what large dining halls are made of.

Washers and dryers are always in great demand as well. A day care centers might be grateful for them.

Even closer to home, many low-income people have non-working or antiquated appliances, and could really use a new one. To find someone who needs your old appliance, check with a senior center. If you don't care who gets it, put it out by the street with a "FREE" and "works good" sign on it, and it will be gone before you know it.

Note: Old *non*-working refrigerators and freezers with Freon must be disposed of at special places. Some communities have collection days once or twice a year when they pick them up free; others have centers where you can bring them in. Some appliance dealers will come out and pick them up and dispose of them for you. Who ever does it, there is usually a charge for the Freon recovery.

Old kitchen appliances (stoves or ranges) from the 1920's '30s and '40s may actually also be valuable because of the "retro" kitchen look being in vogue again. That old relic may be worth a fortune! To see if you can find a buyer, check the Yellow Pages under "Appliances - Major-Used"

If you can't find a taker, your county or city Solid Waste department can advise you about major appliance disposal.

Some people really have a lot, but have no idea how blessed they are.

Kitchen Ware

If the items in question are quality china, crystal or silver, they belong in the estate category and should probably go to an heir.

Everyday dishes, pots and pans, silverware and cooking implements are always in demand by those setting up housekeeping, fire and calamity victims, newlyweds, battered women starting over, and large families.

Shelters, halfway houses, churches, community groups with feeding programs, camps and orphanages all need lots of these items.

Kitchenware when sold in a rummage or garage sale brings only pennies per item, so is far more valuable given to someone who actually needs the dishes and utensils.

Teacups

My cup runneth over...
Psalms 23:5

There is, believe it or not, a teacup ministry that reaches out to women (many in difficult situations) by inviting them to tea, giving them a beautiful teacup and saucer to keep, and letting them know how special they are in God's eyes.

If this is your cup of tea, teacups and saucers (sets only, and no cracked or chipped ones, please), may be sent to Teacup Ministries, P.O. Box 70, Napavine, WA 98565. (360) 740-8287 or contact them via email at (teacup@localaccess.com)

Other China and Dishes

If you have some odd pieces of fine china or dinnerware you might want to sell, contact Replacements, Ltd., 1089 Knox Road, PO Box 26029, Greensboro, NC 27420. (1-800-REPLACE). They sell discontinued and active patterns (thousands of designs) of china, crystal, flatware and collectibles.

Another firm that buys and sells silverware and fine china is Walter Drake, Colorado Springs, CO (get the zip code). There is a continual need for odd pieces by people who want to match their patterns and replace broken pieces or add an additional place setting.

Cleaning Supplies

Nearly all group homes can use cleaning supplies, dishwashing detergent, scouring pads, mops, wax, brooms, buckets and laundry soap. So can many churches, private schools, day care centers and camps. Most are grateful to accept even partial bottles and boxes; just be sure all containers are marked as to contents, particularly strange bottles of unknown contents, which could be detergent, glass cleaner, plant fertilizer or oven cleaner.

Vacuum cleaners, carpet sweepers, shop vacuums, waxers, and buffers are also in demand.

Ironing Boards/Irons

With all the miracle wrinkle-free fabrics there are today, ironing boards and irons aren't the household staples they once were, however most group homes and residential senior centers could still use one or more of these. Also check with whatever local organization helps out families after disasters such as fire, flood, tornado or hurricane.

Cleaning house with children is like shoveling while it snows.

Air Fresheners and Room Deodorizers

These can be used by hospices, convalescent centers, "old folks homes", adult day care centers, old soldiers' homes and any place where there may be incontinent people. They might also be appreciated by fixed-income, homebound caregivers. Your county visiting nurse might know of an appropriate recipient.

Humidifiers, Dehumidifiers, Air Conditioners, Heaters and Air Filters

There are many people to whom the above devices are not luxuries, but life sustaining necessities. Such people might be those with allergies, the elderly who have no central heating, or worse still, no heating at all, or those suffering from the opposite problem, heat prostration in tiny, sweltering apartments.

Give assistance,
not advice in a
crisis.
-Aesop-
(c. 620-560 BC)

People to contact who might know of someone in need of a heating or cooling unit might be the visiting nurse, the advocate at your local senior center, a local pastor or church secretary, or one of the refugee resettlement services.

Chapter Eighteen

COLLECTIONS

The difference between an antique and a collectible is that an antique is generally something that was produced over 100 years ago, and is usually hand wrought. A Collectible can be any age, but usually are of more recent origin. Collectibles frequently start off with little or no intrinsic or artistic value.

The list of things people collect is endless. There are the old traditional favorites: antiques, dolls, stamps, coins, trains, salt and pepper shakers, depression glass, cookie jars, charms for charm bracelets, doll houses, miniatures, plates, clocks, teacups, old glass, and cookbooks, to name but a few.

Then there are the newer "collectibles" which have gained popularity in roughly the last fifty years: Avon containers, Barbie dolls, comic books, numbered edition prints, war souvenirs, model airplanes, political campaign buttons, cars, and videos, even men's duck-bill caps.

Added to that are the obscure things many people don't even realize are collectibles: long-forgotten cans of tennis balls, for instance. The old key-wind cans of Wilson tennis balls today sell for between $15 and $300.

Even old plastic and cardboard charge and credit cards are valuable. An original 1958 American Express cardboard credit card sells for up to $500 today. (Contact: American Credit Card Collectors Society, Box 2465, Midland, MI 48640. (517) 839-2026) to see if your oldies have any value. Even expired phone cards are highly collectible.

Some items that are welcomed by various charities and ministries are foreign currency, postcards, matchbooks and map and shell collections. They will likely sell them to support their mission.

The rule of thumb with collectibles is to get a reliable appraisal or opinion of their value before deciding what to do with them. Some items may not look like much, but could be very valuable. We heard

> **If I hadn't started painting, I would have raised chickens.**
> **-Grandma Moses-**

of one woman who got upset with her son for not cleaning his room, so she threw out his baseball card collection as punishment. She was even more upset when she learned the value of the cards would have financed his college education.

Old comics are especially scarce, because during World War II, comic books were sought after and surrendered to paper drives. That destroyed much of the late 1930's and mid-1940's supply of comics. One old comic book (the first issue of Marvel Comics, published in 1939) recently sold for $35,000.00. A copy of Detective Comics #27, which features the first appearance of Batman in 1939, sold to a collector for $125,000.00.

> Memories, important yesterdays, were once todays. Treasure and notice today.
> -Gloria Gaither-

Authorities Ralph and Terry Kovel have several newsletters and books listing values of collectibles. Contact them at: Kovels on Antiques and Collectibles, ($36/yr.) Box 22900, Beachwood, OH 44122 (800) 829-9158.

Some collections have great sentimental value and should stay within the family (such things as grandpa's old slingshot or peashooter, or his old erector set or the old Lincoln Logs ® all the kids loved to play with.

Some of these little treasures could be contributed to ministries or charities that would sell them and utilize the money. (However if the money is needed, they should be sold by the owner or "disposer" and turned into cash).

Still others, which are discussed in greater detail below, might have even more worth if kept intact and passed on to new, appropriate owners.

Dolls

One word to the wise: Don't let your children or anyone else's, touch any dolls that might be a part of the estate. One young woman executor gave in to her daughter's incessant whining to let her play with the old Barbie dolls among her aunt's estate. Though the dolls were nearly 40 years old, the aunt had never had them out of their original boxes. The Barbies and their boxes were in mint condition.

A few minutes later, the dolls were smudged, the hair was mussed, the clothes wrinkled and dirty, some of the tiny shoes and accessories missing, and the boxes torn and crushed. In that few minutes, the Barbies depreciated in value from being worth hundreds of dollars, to becoming virtually worthless.

Valuable dolls should be treated as part of the estate, while less valuable "play-with" quality dolls might go to little girls in state institutions, homes for the retarded, orphanages, group homes, or schools for the blind.

If you want to put dolls into a ministry, ship them to Jan Crouch at Trinity Broadcasting Network. (2442 Michelle Drive, Tustin, CA 92680.) Each year, Jan takes thousands of dolls overseas to Third World Countries to little girls who have never seen a doll. When the new owners undress their little dollies for the first time, they find a heart sticker on each doll's chest, which says "Jesus Loves You."

If you have valuable dolls you want to sell, you might want to check with Theriaults Antique Doll Auctions, P.O. Box 151, Annapolis, MD 21404. They guarantee not only the best prices for your dolls, but also that they will go to happy homes. They will take one doll or a dozen, or your complete collection. They will take them either through auction consignment or outright purchase. The dolls do not have to be in perfect condition.

They also handle all doll-related items, doll clothes, toys, accessories and teddy bears. They handle all the packing, transportation and insurance for your collection and assist with the shipping. For more information call (800) 638-0422 or check them out on-line at (www.theriaults.com).

Teddy Bears

Police, fire and sheriffs departments need lots of clean new or like-new Teddy Bears. Most officers keep one or two in their patrol cars to help calm distraught children in stressful situations. Police budgets usually don't cover Teddy Bears, and officers frequently end up purchasing the bears themselves.

> we all have our "good old days" tucked away inside our hearts, and we return to them in daydreams like cats to favorite armchairs.
> -Brian Carter-

Please don't feed the Teddy Bears. They're already stuffed.

Because young children tend to chew on, kiss and drool on teddy bears, they're best placed where they will belong to just one child rather than a group.

Children's hospitals usually accept brand new bears. Many state operated facilities for unadopted children could use good bears too. Teddy bears are guaranteed to bring love into a lonely little life.

Even some of the hardened young charges in Juvenile Detention facilities have been known to soften their tough attitudes when given teddy bears.

Most of the above places can also use other stuffed animals as well. If you have stuffed dogs, cats, raccoons, etc., send them along.

Records and Record Players

Many senior centers would welcome a new collection of Golden Oldies, Broadway tunes, dance records, gospel music, western music or timeless classical music. You might only get a few cents for such a record at a used record store, but they'll bring back million dollar memories for many an old timer. They can also probably use a spare record player in case their old faithful gives out.

If you're interested in selling old records and want an idea of value, make a list of what you've got, and send it to:

Magick by Design (Michael Hill)
16575 Stage Stop Road
Falcon, CO 80831-7421
Or email MHill98274@aol.com.

Tapes, CD's, Videos, DVD's and Cassettes

These will find a happy home with young people, the bed-ridden, lonely teenagers, seniors in rehabilitation centers and military personnel overseas. Christian tapes (sermons and music) are comforting to AIDS patients, the dying in nursing homes, missionaries, and many ministries. (Among them, Widow's Mite, page 206)

Stamp Collections

There are two types of stamp collections: very valuable and hobby quality. Only an appraiser can tell the difference. A valuable collection can either be treated as a part of the inheritance and passed on to the family member or friend who would most appreciate it, or it can be sold, and the proceeds be put into the estate.

A less valuable collection might be a wonderful life-long gift to a younger family member who might have shown an interest in it at some time.

If you have no takers in the immediate family, the following groups seek stamps:

Shriner's Children's Hospital of Northern California
2425 Stockton Boulevard
Sacramento, CA 95817

Shriners wants colorful (but not valuable) used postage stamps to put to use in keeping some very sick children preoccupied.

Father Flanagan's Boy's Home
Attn: Stamp Center
129 S. 144ᵗʰ Street
Boys Town, NE 68010

Father Flanagan Girls and Boys Town funds many of their youth programs through the sale of donated stamps and coins. They are particularly interested in receiving mounted collections (both U.S. and foreign) and U.S. mint stamps in sheets and blocks. They also have a great need for philatelic literature for their reference library. They accept almost all kinds of philatelic and numismatic material, but cannot accept bulk shipments without prior confirmation that the donation is something they can use.

Material should be securely packed. You should make up a reasonable inventory list and include the appraisal if the value is over $5,000. With a large collection, list only a description such as "One Volume Collection of 20ᵗʰ Century U.S. Mint Stamps, 1935-1975."

> Be like a postage stamp – stick to one thing until you get there.
> -Josh Billings-

A copy of the list (including your name and address) should be placed in the shipping box. You may call the Stamp Center Manager at (402) 498-1143 with any questions.

A Canadian group that would appreciate donations of stamps is:

Canadian Guide Dogs for the Blind
4120 Rideau Valley Drive North
P.O. Box 290
Manotick, Ontario K4M 1A3
(613) 692-7777

CGDB collects all types of used stamps: special issues, regular stamps, U.S., Canadian and foreign stamps.

There are some general rules that apply to saving any stamps: leave at least ¼" of paper around the stamp. This protects the perforations. If the perforated edge is damaged, the stamp is valueless. A stamp is also worthless if it has been torn, creased or has a very black cancellation mark, a pencil or ballpoint pen mark, tape or any other paper affixed to the stamp.

Shell Collections

Are there seashell collectors? Are there ever! Conchologists of America love to get new additions to their vast collection. They accept donations under the following terms and conditions:

I have a large seashell collection. I keep it scattered on beaches all over the world. Maybe you've seen it?

1. They cannot agree to keep all the material in a collection. (They receive many duplicates of existing holdings). They use donations for teaching materials, museum displays and occasional sales.

2. They cannot guarantee they will keep an individual's collection together.

3. They cannot agree to put something on display in perpetuity. They have fourteen million specimens, so only the smallest fraction will ever be on display.

4. The donor must have acquired all donated specimens legally. (Laws for collecting specimens are becoming stricter and more complex.)

5. To donate shell collections, contact:

    Conchologist of America
    Department of Mollusks
    Academy of Natural Sciences
    1900 Benjamin Franklin Parkway
    Philadelphia, PA 19103-1195

Cookie Jars

Cookie jars are frequently associated with being a place to hide money, not being valuable items themselves. But many are very valuable and they don't even have to be really old to be worth quite a bit! Even jars from as recently as the 1970's are sought by collectors. The California Originals Company's Big Bird brings $52 and Eeyore $185. Star Wars collectors are happy to pay $85 for R2D2 and C3PO goes for $135.

The Cookie Jar: Grandma's favorite hiding place for when she "kneaded a little extra dough."

If no young person in the family has an interest in the jar, perhaps a group home could use it. If it is valuable, perhaps the best choice is to sell it and give the money to your favorite charity.

Really Obscure Collections

It seems like no matter what object you can think of, somebody, somewhere, collects it and would love to add your collection to his or her own. The best way to find your fellow collectors is to do an Internet search.

Some collectors are individuals, some are universities or professional organizations, and others are government entities. If in doubt, don't throw it out – until you at least have someone conduct an Internet search.

Professional and Business Memorabilia

Many businesses and industries maintain museums or collections of early artifacts, tools and papers of their trade. The objectives of most are acquiring, cataloging, documenting, preserving, storing and exhibiting items from the early days of their existence. Many even have staffs of curators, restorers, catalogers and researchers, all devoted to finding, collecting and preserving more items. Most are virtual museums of the ingenuity of America.

One man who took the challenge to preserve his papers seriously was TV's Dan Rather, who sent a quarter million items to Boston University over a 36-year period. His stuff included everything from an Emmy Award to paper scraps. Few institutions could or would accept a collection of that size.

I must say that acting was good training for the political life that lay ahead of us. -Nancy Reagan-

On the other side of the coin are thousands of people who were a part of America's business or manufacturing history, but who have no idea of the significance of their contribution. If you were a pioneer or old-timer in an industry, track down the museum or collection that covers your background, call them, and if nothing else, tell them who you are and what you did, and ask if they are interested in interviewing you. Most have vast interview tapes (called "oral histories"), which are used by researchers to piece together all the little details of the history of the industry.

You may hold the missing piece to one of their puzzles. They are also interested in your story if you took part in a famous event, or knew or worked with a noteworthy person.

There are dozens of old time local telephone museums, mining museums, and teacher's museums in addition to museums established by companies, such as the Boeing Museum of Flight. The latter museum was the recent recipient of 16 boxes of objects and archival material from a man who had visited the museum and was so impressed with their collection that he included them in his will.

This was a perfect win – win situation. An even better solution is to give your collection while you're alive. The beauty of giving to a museum is that you can go visit your stuff any time you want to.

Chapter Nineteen

HOBBIES

Pianos, Organs and Electronic Keyboards

There are so many worthy potential recipients you'll be wishing you had more than one instrument to dispose of. For starters, think of churches, senior centers, schools, camps, youth symphonies, or some young person who has shown a musical talent or real interest in learning to play.

> Music hath charms to sooth the savage beast.
> -William Congreve, 1670-1729-

An electronic keyboard is a lot easier to carry around than a piano. This might be a fine item for a group, church or ministry with a prison outreach. You might even consider a college student who can't take the family piano with him. Kids raised with a piano really miss them when away at school.

If you're donating a very valuable piano, have it appraised and get a receipt. That way you can possibly claim it as a charitable contribution (depending upon the donee). Also with pianos, take into account the cost to move it, as well as the tuning and servicing it will need in its new location. Is this part of your gift, or should the recipient make these arrangements?

Other Musical Instruments

Many smaller school districts and private Christian schools have no budget for musical instruments, and would welcome contributions of instruments for use by the school band or in music classes or lessons. Donated instruments become the property of the school district, and students can check out an instrument the same way they do a library book.

Also check with local colleges, private music schools, private dance studios or preschools to find out whether or not their programs can use your instrument. You may also want to check with a service club such as the VFW or American Legion. One especially worthy group that needs bugles is Bugles

Across America. These are folks who volunteer to play TAPS at veteran's funerals. Their address is on page 234.

Don't forget about individuals. There may be someone in your family, a friend's child, or someone you know at work who could put the instrument to years of good use. Young people who loved listening to your play and showed a genuine appreciation for your music might also be good recipients. Perhaps he or she might develop into a future virtuoso.

> There's many a good tune played on an old fiddle.
> -Samuel Butler-

Would-be donors whose musical instruments are damaged or out of tune needn't worry. Most music teachers are adept at making repairs and tuning instruments.

Many churches these days have orchestras, and most Senior Centers would also appreciate musical instruments for dancing and other activities. All the above groups can also likely use anything else related to the subject, such as sheet music, music stands, music stand lights, music manuscript paper and risers (collapsible and permanent).

In Minneapolis, a group called Wonderful World of Music (612) 922-2121 takes musical instruments, sends them to Red Wing Technical College to be restored, then gives them to young people who can't afford new instruments. There may be a similar program in your area. A call to the music teacher at your local junior or senior high or technical college may produce results.

Sheet Music, Music Books

The only known public library in the world whose sole purpose is to lend sheet music resides safely in a large barn in Maine. It is the Bagaduce Music Lending Library, and claims over 150,000 titles covering keyboard, solo and small-ensemble instrumental, pop and classical vocal, secular and sacred choral, opera and musical theater scores, and other categories of all eras.

Their entire collection for the most part has been donated by retiring performers, composers, teachers, from estates, and amateur musicians. Whatever the source, they welcome and treasure it all.

They also have an extensive collection of books about music, biographies, musicology, music analysis, histories, music encyclopedias and music theory texts. They also make these available for research and study.

They accept music donations of all kinds including a few instruments. (They also loan instruments on occasion).

Bagaduce Music Lending Library
3 Music Library Lane
Blue Hill, ME 04614
(207) 374-5454
www.bagaducemusic.org

Arts and Crafts Supplies

You'll have no trouble finding a home for arts and crafts supplies. Senior centers, youth groups, schools, camps, Sunday Schools and missionaries will take all you have. Most have program directors that are experts at "making something from nothing."

How many beautiful projects lie hidden in these old "makings"?

Many senior groups make crafts items all year long and hold sales periodically to come up with spare money to fund little extras. Such groups usually sell their wares at the county fair, or at Christmas bazaars. You can make contact with them in those places, and find potential recipients for your donation of crafts "makings."

Camping Supplies

Tents, sturdy rain gear, sleeping bags, backpacks, lanterns, cots, compasses, bug sprays, coolers, Thermos jugs, area trail maps and outdoor cooking gear can be used by Scout troops, youth camps or a struggling family who might enjoy an outdoor experience but can't afford the initial expense.

Outdoor gear could also be used by youth groups (particularly low-income or inner city groups), and search and rescue units. The Salvation Army also conducts extensive day and summer camp programs in most areas of the country.

There are also many farms and ranches for troubled youth who have gotten into hot water with the law. Most give the kids a healthy dose of country living, hard work, working with animals and communing with nature. They can always use more camping supplies.

Finally, there are those who commune with nature on a daily basis - the homeless. Living and surviving in the elements isn't a fun experience for them, so any camping supplies would probably be appreciated. The problem is contacting them, since most are nomads. Start by checking with a mission or men's center and let them distribute what it is you have to give.

Fishing Collectibles

Give a man a fish and you feed him for a day; teach a man to fish and he'll eat forever. -Chinese Proverb-

Dad's old tackle box may contain more value than his safe deposit box. The market for old fishing gear is thriving. It doesn't matter whether it's old lures, rods, reels, creels or hand-tied fishing flies (Ask a fisherman whether yours are hand-tied.) If they are and your want to sell them, advertise with: *The Old Reel Collectors' Association Newsletter,* 200 State Road, 206 E., St. Augustine, FL 32086, (904) 692-2037 or *National Fishing Lure Collectors Club Gazette,* Box 13, Grove City, OH 43123.

Games and Puzzles

Who can use the gift of diversion? People whose hearts and minds are heavy with grief or worry, those who must occupy children while someone is in the hospital, those who must while away lonely hours, or the lonely who must keep their minds active to ward off vegetation.

Games and puzzles can always be used by veterans hospitals or children's hospitals, old soldiers' homes, prisons, Ronald McDonald Houses, drug and alcohol rehabilitation centers, senior centers, orphanages, detention homes, pre-schools, private schools and some camps.

Checkers, chess, puzzles, pick-up sticks, mazes and various contraptions of mental dexterity can be used both for entertainment as well as teaching mental skills and coordination.

Hobby Train Sets

Miniature trains sets could be hobbies, collectibles or both.

Within every man lives a little boy, and vice versa.

Many men who own trains have invested thousands of hours and dollars in building and maintaining elaborate villages and sets to surround them. Most are in the category of valuable collectibles rather than toys. An unsupervised child or two turned loose with them could destroy them in no time.

On the other hand, if there's a special grandson or granddaughter who lovingly shared those hundreds of hours enjoying the trains with Grandpa, perhaps he or she is the best recipient. (But do they have space for the room full of "village"?) Perhaps the set could be boxed up and stored for them until they are adults.

If wanting to dispose of the set outside the family, a quick analysis is first necessary. If the "village" is a miniature duplication of the local town or area, then a local historical society or museum would probably welcome it. The beauty of this type of donation is that then many people would get the opportunity to enjoy it.

A Boys Home or facility for orphaned or troubled young men might also be good recipients, since it would be used and enjoyed under supervision.

If you have some rare or classic model trains in your collection, you might even consider loaning or donating them to the National Toy Train Museum, (717) 687-8976, 300 Paradise Lane, Strasburg, PA 17589.

If all else fails, sell it. Check with train magazines for potential buyers, or run an ad. There are many such magazines. Among them are: Classic Toy Trains, Model Railroader, Model Train Magazine, O-Gauge Magazine, Railroad Model Craftsman and Live Steam to name a few. Some old Lionel electric train sets now sell for thousands of dollars.

Other potential buyers might include one of the many railroad themed restaurants popular around the country. These establishments have model trains running overhead among all the diners.

Photography and Dark Room Equipment

Most schools, whether vocational or technical schools, community college, high schools or junior highs, would jump at the opportunity to own photo and dark room equipment. So would groups or organizations that teach vocational skills to young people, such as scout groups, organizations that publish newspapers, or perhaps a budding young photographer.

Slides, Old Movies and Snapshots

"Who in the world would want my old travel slides, or movies of life back on the farm?" you might wonder. You'd be surprised at what a hot commodity they might be.

In response to a small item in a local paper asking if anyone would be interested in such items, three teachers called, hoping to get the slides as teaching tools for history and social studies, people from two different arts organizations thought they would be good "creativity sparkers" and a man who puts on slide shows in nursing homes and senior centers wanted them.

Nature composes
some of her
loveliest poems for
the microscope
and the
telescope.
-Theodore Roszak-

Telescopes, Binoculars, Magnifying Glasses and Microscopes

Many small or impoverished school districts would love to have such equipment. So would many private schools, Christian schools and home school organizations. A budding astronomer or scientist might also be a good choice too. A local science teacher might know of a worthy candidate. If it's a really valuable professional quality item, you might offer it as a prize to the student who writes the best paper on: astronomy (telescope), biology (microscope) or birds (binoculars). Let the science teacher set up the rules, run the contest and pick the winner. Having to work and compete to get it will make it even more valuable to the young person who wins it.

Such items might also be appreciated by medical students (microscope), bird watchers (binoculars) and senior centers (telescope and magnifying glasses).

Sewing Machines

Remember Motel the young tailor in *Fiddler on the Roof*? His dream was for a sewing machine so he could marry Tzeitel and make a living as a tailor. That story still holds true. A sewing machine can still make a person a good living as a tailor, a seamstress, a small clothing manufacturer, by doing alterations, or by upholstering furniture. One of the refugee resettlement organizations might know of an immigrating tailor with a similar dream.

It might also pay to check with small or poor school districts who might be able to use the machine in their home economics class, or with vocational or trade schools in your area.

Others who might be able to put a sewing machine to good use are group homes and missionaries.

Fabrics, Fabric Scraps, Rags, Patterns, and Sundries

There's a whole subculture of ladies behind the closed doors of America who lovingly manufacture a lifetime supply of quilts for their families, friends, and frequently even casual acquaintances who happen to mention that they like quilts. These nice, nurturing ladies utilize miles of fabric in their quest to see that everyone they know sleeps warm.

When you get lemons, make lemonade, but when life gives you scraps, make quilts.

Many a garment has had several lives, first perhaps as a dress or drape, then reused to create accessories or parts for smaller or other outfits, doll clothes, quilt tops, pot holders or "stuffing" (filler) for some other project. Such thrift isn't as commonplace today as it was several decades ago, but there are still many women who can't look at a piece of fabric without envisioning enough projects to utilize every last thread of it.

"There's hardly a piece of fabric so small that it can't be made into something beautiful by a quilter."

There are many community quilting societies that create and raffle collector quilts to raise money for non-profit organizations. To donate quilting scraps, keep an eye open for mention of them, or run a small ad in your little thrifty paper and let the quilters find you. You can also find a quilter's group near you by calling the American Quilter's Society at 502-898-7903.

Even really stained clothing or fabric still has a use. Rag merchants pay a penny a pound for "reject" clothing or fabric. They then compress it into bales and sell it either as clothing for Third World countries, or as industrial wiping rags or mattress filler.

Look in your local Yellow Pages under "Rags" or "Wiping Cloths" for contacts in your area.

One ministry that collects fabrics and sewing notions for distribution overseas is World Concern. They always have a critical need for fabric (minimum 1/4 yard) and any boxed or bagged sewing supplies such as thread, needles, buttons, scissors, and notions of all kinds.

World Concern Supply Service
19802 Highway 99
Lynnwood, WA 98036
1-800-755-5022

Chapter Twenty

SPORTING GOODS

Ball and other Game Supplies

Baseballs, bats and mitts, soccer balls, footballs and basketballs will be easy to dispose of. Virtually any youth group can use them. Before giving them away though, be sure none are of the antique variety. Old autographed baseballs are in great demand, and pre-World War II baseball mitts labeled with the name of a hall-of-famer are worth real money. For example a Babe Ruth Home Run Special from about 1927 recently sold for $2,475. When it was new it sold for $6 - $8.

Even unlabeled models or unusual mitt designs are valuable if they're in good shape. For further info check with:

> He who really wants a toy does not care whether it is perfect or not.

The Glove Collector
14057 Rolling Hills Lane
Dallas, TX 75240
(214) 699-1808.

Bicycles, Motorbikes and ATV's

In these days of frequent litigation by careless, ungrateful or dishonest recipients of such items, it might be prudent to donate the bikes, etc. to a charity or ministry, and let *them* pick the recipient rather than you giving them directly to the chosen owner. Many youth groups, group homes and camps would welcome such items.

Exercise Equipment

Many seniors are really into keeping fit these days, and the local senior center might be glad to add your equipment to their workout room. Many rehabilitation programs and community clubs also have exercise equipment, (as do many churches) and most could always use more.

Golf Clubs and Golf Carts

Golf clubs are frequently used by camps (particularly boys' camps), boys' homes, local schools that might want to put together a school team but lack funding and equipment, some inner-city groups, a few senior centers, and many rehabilitation programs. Some smaller cities with inadequately funded sports programs may be able to use them as loaners or for use during classes.

Golf carts and wheeled golf bag carriers can be used by even more groups: camps, homes and ranches for troubled youth, handicapped programs, old soldiers' or disabled veterans' hospitals, drug and alcohol rehabilitation farms, some senior service providers, some church organizations, or any organization with several spread-out buildings that require people to carry things back and forth.

On the civic side, park departments, county fairgrounds, and community golf courses could also use them. Some schools and job training programs could probably use them too.

The homeless could use wheeled golf bag carts too in case of frequently stolen grocery store carts.

A man's got to do what a man's got to do. (Clean out the garage.)

Old Trophies

Just as old trophies gave recognition and pride to their original recipients, they can do the same job again and again for new owners with the simple change of a fresh nameplate. Many under-funded sports teams, junior bowling leagues, and small school districts with no budget for sports are ideal recipients.

If the trophy is for a particularly noteworthy achievement, then perhaps it should pass on to the school, team, or institution of which it was a part. If there is a museum honoring the sport, perhaps the trophy should reside there. (The Baseball or Football Hall of Fame, for instance.)

Skis, Sleds, Skates and Snowboards

These paraphernalia of winter sports can be used by a number of groups. Look for those who provide winter snow fun for inner city youth, church groups, the handicapped and Special Olympics participants. A local ski shop will usually know who runs such programs and needs gear.

Such groups need cold weather clothing too: sweaters, jackets, ski pants or ski bibs, ski boots, mittens, gloves, wool caps, long underwear and scarves.

Swimming Pool Supplies

Organizations with pools that might be able to use pool supplies are camps, YMCA and YWCA's, schools, rehabilitation centers, some senior centers, and community centers. Be sure all containers of chemicals are clearly marked as to contents, directions for use and quantities.

Water Skis and Waterfront equipment

Pool chairs, lounges, life vests, a spare diving board, pool chemicals, pool toys or a pool vacuum cleaner, beach towels, or cabanas would surely be welcomed by any group with a pool or pool program.

Water skis, jet skis, and ski boats require large bodies of water rather than pools, but there are dozens of worthy groups around who would gladly take them off your hands.

Potential recipients include summer camps, scout camps, Salvation Army programs, search and rescue groups, marine patrols and rehabilitation programs that teach self-reliance through water programs.

Sports Paraphernalia

When cleaning out piles of magazines, don't finally throw out those old game programs you've been storing for years. Vintage sports programs are a hot commodity! So are old game tickets and ticket stubs. If you have a program from one of the old Negro League games, from before Jackie Robinson integrated the major leagues, for instance, you can probably start packing for that trip to the Caribbean you've wanted to take.

Been there, done that. (Now get rid of the stuff!)

Chapter Twenty-One

OFFICE EQUIPMENT

Audio/Video Equipment and Accessories

This category includes television sets, radios, VCR's, DVD's, tape recorders, tapes, movie cameras, projectors, movies, slide projectors and slides, projection screens, and CD burners.

Virtually all of the above items communicate and educate. Consider giving them to schools: private, public, pre- schools, home-school organizations, and trade schools.

They also can be put to use by many types of group homes such as those for senior citizens, youth, runaway shelters, halfway houses, drug and alcohol rehabilitation homes and hospices. Such organizations as Mothers Against Violence can also use them, as can career training or retraining groups.

If their condition is marginal or in need of repair, your local trade school might be glad to get them so students can learn to repair and rehabilitate them.

Copy Machines, Duplicators & Printing Presses

These are basic equipment for most organizations, be they non-profit, church, civic or educational groups. These are more items that will have so many potential takers, you may find yourself wishing you had a dozen to give away.

It costs only a few pennies to make a copy. Think of the poor Monks who copied the whole Bible by hand.

This may be one decision best left to your heart. Do you want to have it used to communicate the Gospel by giving it to a missionary or church? Should it go to a "patriot," political or civic organization? Or perhaps to a school or a lone individual who works tirelessly from his/her home on one crusade or another and needs to be able to duplicate press releases and flyers?

This is also a category that is ideal for the exercise of letting the recipient come to you. This process is described on page 203.

Personal Computers & Computer Equipment

With the average life span of computers rapidly decreasing to two years or less, the estimated number being disposed of is expected to reach half a billion units by the year 2007.

Even obsolete computer equipment (and most of it is within a few months of purchasing it) is welcomed by many under-funded groups or institutions. Schools tend to want only the latest up-to-date computers, but not so with many churches and other non-profit operations.

Even though it may have cost thousands of dollars originally, computer equipment will bring virtually nothing on the resale market. Thus it is best to give it to a group or person who will use it and be grateful for it, even if it isn't the last word in technology.

Many cities have "used computer banks" which refurbish old computers and give them to charities and worthy individuals. One such bank in Seattle is 1-206-365-4657. Another in the Pacific Northwest is Computer Recycling, (206) 296-8800 (On the Internet, they're at http://dnr.metrokc.gov/swd/crp.htm)

One national ministry that could use late model computers is St. Judes Ranch for Children, P.O. Box 60100, Boulder City, NV 89006-0100. (800) 492-3562.

Others who need used computers are inner-city youth groups, after-school babysitting programs, missionaries and a host of others.

Really old computers (some of the very early models) have finally come to be treasured as historical artifacts. One collector, Sellam Ismail, is a computer historian and consultant who owns more than 1,500 models and runs the semi-annual Vintage Computer Festival. http://www.vintage.org).

Most prices are generally still low — $5 to $100 for computers that originally cost thousands of dollars. However, on ebay (http://www.ebay.com) over 100 aged computers showed up in a search for "vintage computers," with asking prices as high as $1,999.

> I think there is a world market for maybe five computers.
> -Thomas Watson, chairman of IBM, 1943-

Rare ones can be worth a fortune, especially if they are complete, in working condition, and come with related accessories and software. Before disposing of the old relic computer elsewhere, do an ebay search and perhaps list it there.

If you still can't find any takers, computer-recycling suggestions are on page 156.

Old Computer Printers

According to SmartBusinessMag.com, there are 90 million printers in use in the U.S. Laser printers have an average 6-year lifespan while inkjet printers last only about 3 years. Like their companion computers, there will be many charities and individuals grateful for a printer of any kind.

Old empty HP toner cartridges can be taken to Mail Boxes, Etc., who will ship them back to the manufacturer at no charge to you. Hewlett Packard has recycled 12-million toner cartridges since 1990.

Keep in mind that having the latest word in printers isn't a priority to someone who may have none at all. Perhaps a struggling family who has a computer but no printer would grateful for one.

Office Equipment and Office Supplies

This category consists of things like desks, chairs, file cabinets, file folders, paper, pens, pencils, erasers, staplers, rulers, tape dispensers, dry eraser boards or blackboards, coffee makers, coffee cups and lunch room dishes, adding machines, standard typewriters, paper shredders, and all the little paraphernalia that is used in an office. Virtually every type of organization can use anything you care to give. (Standard typewriters are becoming rare and valued for typing job applications and forms that can't be done easily by computer.)

> A place for everything and everything in its place.
> -Samuel Smiles (1812-1904)-

Occasionally a school will adopt a "sister school" in some third world country, and one of the things it usually does is send boxes of school supplies, pens and paper. Inconceivable as it may sound, many people in this world have never owned a pencil.

Many under-funded school districts that no longer supply such items to their students can use the basics, - pencils, pens and paper. Day care centers can always use paper (plain paper, construction paper, copy machine, colored, or old tractor-feed stock). Vocational Education training programs for handicapped people and "special ed" job training classes in public schools can use envelopes and obsolete printed letterheads for classroom training programs. (They practice stuffing and sorting bulk mailings. Once trained they can be paid or volunteer at non-profit charities that do lots of mailings).

Overhead Projector

You can pick just about any organization on our list for this one. Whether used for teaching, preaching or just illustrating points, there's hardly an organization, school or church that can't use an overhead projector.

Telephones, FAX and Answering Machines

Even the ring of the phone brings hope to one and fears to another.

Today, thirty million wireless phones lay idle and discarded, with most eventually headed for the dumpster. This creates a potential environmental problem, since mobile phones contain toxic materials such as cadmium, lead, mercury and gallium arsenide. By recycling these mobile phones back into re-use, this environmental damage can be averted.

Most groups with an office can always use another telephone. Schools, neighborhood watch groups, Crisis hotlines and Christian counseling ministries can use them too. So can special education classes for use in teaching life skills.

Domestic Abuse groups especially treasure cell phones. They are distributed to women who are in dangerous and abusive situations and need cell phone for their safety.

To donate your used cell phone to help fight domestic violence, mail the phone, battery and charger to:

The Wireless Foundation
CALL to PROTECT, c/o Motorola
1580 E. Ellsworth Road
Ann Arbor, MI 48108

If you would like a receipt for tax purposes, be sure to include a written request with your name and address. The Wireless Foundation is a non-profit 501c3 organization, so shipping costs is tax deductible as well.

Don't throw out that clunky old cell phone. It will be welcomed by many groups

Be sure to shut your service off before donating the phone so you don't end up with an unexpected phone bill.

On a larger scale, CARE and Collective Good International collects donated mobile phones in North America and re-deploys them back into use overseas. CARE reaches out to people whose lives are devastated by disasters in 60 countries in Africa, Asia, Europe and Latin America.

Some of the phones will be used by CARE's in-country field staffs to more efficiently perform their aid, development and relief efforts. The remaining phones will be refurbished by CollectiveGood, and recycled back into use. In most countries, the majority of the citizens have never enjoyed the benefits of telecommunications. These phones provide affordable first-time modern communications at a fraction of the cost of new phones (which are priced out of the reach of the average Third World citizen).

Send the used Phone(s) with any extra accessories (extra batteries, charging unit, automobile power plug, case, etc.) to:

CollectiveGood, Inc.
Charity Code 28-CARE
1440 Rough Creek Road
London, KY 40744

You will receive an acknowledgement letter from CARE for this donation.

High Tech Stuff

Not everyone has high tech surveillance gear to dispose of, but in case you do, one organization that could use it is American Border Patrol. This is a civilian organization that assists the Immigration Service in tracking and apprehending aliens coming into our country illegally.

They need GPS units (Magellan, Garmin, etc.), high-powered binoculars, Digital cameras video and still, field communications equipment, night vision goggles, computers (Windows XL and Apple OS 9.0 +), satellite telephones. Software (for video editing and photo editing) and satellite dishes and receivers

They can also use aircraft and Off-road vehicles (4 wheel drive, ATVs, etc.).

American Border Patrol
2160 E Fry Blvd #426
Sierra Vista, AZ 85635
1-800-600-8642
For more information, log on to
http://www.americanpatrol.org/

Chapter Twenty-Two

HOLIDAY & SPECIAL OCCASION ITEMS

Special Christmas Treasures

Christmas is the key time of year in many people's lives, even non-believers in the One whose birthday it celebrates. We move heaven and earth to come "home" for Christmas if at all possible; to share gifts, a big turkey dinner, marvel at how the kids have all grown, and above all, share our love with our families, and thank the Lord for giving us all another year of life. It is the most sentimental of our holidays. Because of that, virtually everything we own that's a Christmas item has strong sentimental value, whether it's a special Christmas ornament, the turkey platter, or the old gift wrap you carefully refold and use year after year.

If there are such treasures among the things to be disposed of, keep these special items in the family. If "little Timmy" especially loved the angel on the top of the tree, perhaps now 50-year old Tim would like it to pass on to his great-grandchildren. The same might be true of other special tree ornaments, table or wall decorations, and special dinnerware used only at the Christmas dinner.

We know of one young lady who, when asked which of her grandmother's many valuable possessions she would want most, without hesitation picked Grandma's Christmas dishes. Just the thought of the wonderful meals she enjoyed off those plates set her to salivating. That china was obviously destined to be a family heirloom.

Other Christmas Things

Once the valuable Christmas things have been divided among various family members and friends, there will still be other things left: wrapping paper, fancy boxes, the tree stand, ornaments and miscellaneous decorations and Christmas cards.

> I wish we could put up some of the Christmas spirit in jars and open a jar of it every month.
> -Harlan Miller (Better Homes & Gardens)

147

Many groups who try to provide Christmas for those without families can use those. Start by checking with churches, senior centers, institutions that house people, youth homes, homeless shelters, and shelters for abused women and unwed mothers.

Christmas Trees

Artificial trees can be used by just about any group home or facility, or perhaps an individual or family who can't afford one. Salvation Army would probably be able to suggest a good recipient.

But who would believe that a cut Christmas tree would be as valuable after Christmas as it is prior to December 25?

They truly are to many communities, but probably nowhere more so than to the people of Louisiana. The state of Louisiana loses 30 miles of coastline each year to erosion. There, old Christmas trees are used to break the wave action and restore their coastal marshes. The trees are placed in wire "corrals" to protect the coastline from salt-water intrusion. The corrals now span a mile, and contain over a million Christmas trees. There are 4.1 million acres of marsh on Louisiana's southern border, and the grateful Louisianans prove there's a new life in the dead trees saving their wetlands.

Locally, most cities or counties now pick up old Christmas trees and grind them into free compost and mulch for use in city and county parks.

Greeting Cards - New

Most people keep a small supply of cards, — greeting cards, thank you, birthday, Christmas and other special occasion cards. These would be welcomed by many people who can't get out to shop for cards for one reason or another, but who still would love to remember friends or loved ones with cards.

New cards can be used by those in prisons, subsidized senior housing centers, Veteran's hospitals and Old Soldiers' Homes, homes for the retarded and disabled, mental health institutions, homes for unwed mothers, and various rehabilitation shelters.

One final note about giving new cards: Donate a few stamps, too. They are really needed and appreciated by residents, many of whom are destitute and live in what amounts to a "cashless" society.

Greeting Cards - Used

Many group homes, particularly those with child-like residents, have a continuing need for used cards of all types, — birthday cards, valentines and Christmas cards.

Used greeting cards can also be used for crafts projects by Sunday School and nursery school classes, scout groups, older adult daycare centers, and low-income day camps. Many group home clients "recycle" used cards by making them into new "cards" and gift tags, which they sell to help with their support and to raise pin money.

One group that gladly takes all the cards they can get is:

Greeting cards can have multiple lives if sent to the right groups.

St. Jude's Ranch for Children
100 St. Jude Street, Boulder City
Nevada 89005-1618.

Send just the front picture portion of both greeting cards and Christmas cards to them, and they'll make the old cards into new ones.

Chapter Twenty-Three

RECYCLING

Recycling Guidelines

If you're fortunate enough to live in a city or county that offers periodic mega-recycling events for big items, count your blessings and use the opportunity to get rid of your old "dead" refrigerator, washer or hard to dispose of items.

If disposing of things like used automobile oil or antifreeze, leftover paint, cleaning supplies, drain openers and other hazardous chemicals, take the products in their original containers, or have them clearly labeled as to contents. Unmarked contents will have to be tested, and that vastly increases the disposal cost.

Putting perfectly good items back into their intended or even expanded use, is the ultimate in recycling.

In order for recycling to work, items recycled must be clean. Rinse bottles and cans and remove bottle caps and lids.

Items that *Can* Be Recycled

Batteries

Automotive batteries

Alkaline batteries. Nearly everything from cell phones to power tools now run on nickel-cadmium batteries. In fact, 95% of U.S. Households own some type of Ni-Cad powered product. These batteries should not go in the trash. There are 29,000 recycling spots nationwide. To find the closest one, call 1-800-822-8837 or visit the Rechargeable Battery Recycling Corp. site at (www.rbrc.org). (This site also has tips on making your batteries last longer.)

Cans

Aluminum pop, beer and juice cans and tin food cans

Pop Can Pull Tabs

In 1989 at the Elora Branch of the Royal Canadian Legion, one man, Ray Pearse, heard a rumor that 10,000 aluminum pop tabs could be sold to earn enough money to buy a wheelchair. He collected he required number of tabs, but then found out the wheelchair rumor wasn't true. However he turned that myth into reality. By 1992 he had collected enough tabs to buy two wheelchairs. Then he teamed up with the Canadian Girl Guides who took on the project. To date they have collected enough tabs to buy over 400 battery-powered wheelchairs.

The tabs are pure aluminum but they're more like pure gold to the charities that collect them. It takes 1,267 tabs to make one pound of pure aluminum, and that brings the charity 40-50 cents. But those tabs, and those pennies, add up. It takes about 4 million tabs to buy one electric wheelchair.

In the U.S. most Ronald McDonald Houses collect the tabs and use the money to pay electric and utility bills. Call the Ronald McDonald House closest to your community to see if they have a Pop Tab collection program.

Many Ronald McDonald Houses provide cardboard collection containers in the shape of a little house. Drop-off sites range in location from McDonald's restaurants to local banks, grocery stores, and in some areas, Toys R Us stores. (Just don't mail them. It wouldn't be cost effective because the cost of the postage would be more than the value of the tabs.

Some organizations also collect the tabs to finance kidney dialysis. Check with your local Kidney Foundation.

Glass Bottles (place in glass only bins)
> Brown bottles (no lids)
> Clear bottles (no lids)
> Green bottles (no lids)
> Jars (no food residue)

Paper

Cardboard, catalogs, cereal Boxes, computer paper, envelopes (windows OK), junk mail, magazines, newspapers, (all sections and inserts), and phone books.

Plastic Bottles (#1 & #2 only)

#1 bottles are usually liquor bottles, peanut butter jars, soda bottles and wine bottles.

#2 bottles are usually detergent bottles, milk jugs, shampoo bottles and water bottles.

Polyurethane Foam

Polyurethane foam (such as couch cushions, carpet padding and prime upholstery padding) has open cells (like a sponge). It must be dry and free of debris and cloth. Check your Yellow Pages under "recycling – Urethane."

Plastic Packing Peanuts

Drop off extra Styrofoam pellets or "packing peanuts" at local private mailing centers such as your neighborhood Mail Boxes, Etc. They'll reuse them. You can also call the Plastic Loosefill Products Council (1-800-828-2214) for the names of other local businesses that re-use them.

If you must throw them out, please bag them securely before putting them in the trash. They make a terrible mess if they get loose in the wind.

Plastic Grocery Bags

Plastic grocery bags can be recycled at nearly every grocery store, and many thrift stores are glad to get them, because they re-use them. If you want to give them another life, they can also be used by Widow's Mite Mission (page 206)

The truth of the matter is that you always know the right thing to do. The hard part is doing it.
-Norman Schwarzkopf-

Tires

Many tire shops will take old tires in for recycling. If there's enough tread left on them, they may even re-sell them. They take automobile, truck, and semi tires (with and without rims).

Used Motor Oil

"Cleanliness is next to Godliness" it is said, though not by the Bible. I seriously doubt the golden streets are laden with trash as are the earth's.

Motor oil is very recyclable. Oil doesn't wear out, it just gets dirty. Go to (www.cleanup.org) and enter your zip code to find an oil recycling facility near you.

Yard Waste Recyclables

These include grass, leaves, weeds, fruit and vegetables that have not been cooked, branches up to four inches in diameter (must usually be bundled in 2' wide by 4' long bundles) and Christmas trees.

Special compostable bags must frequently be used for yard waste recycling. Plastic bags are not compostable. Check with the recycling company in your area to see what must be used.

Also recyclable in some areas (but not all) are wood scraps, stumps, scraps, concrete, brick, drywall, asphalt, roofing and paint (but no creosote or lead-based paint.)

Many recycling centers will not take dirt, sod or rocks.

Items that *Can Not* be Recycled

(Place in Trash Cans)

Non-Recyclable Paper

Carbon paper

Cereal box liners

Containers with food residue

Disposable diapers

Drink boxes

Foil wrapping paper

Frozen food boxes

Ice cream cartons

Paper napkins, towels, plates & cups

Pizza boxes (take-out)

Plastic coated paper

Tissues and toilet paper

Wax coated cardboard, cartons or paper

Non-Recyclable Cans and Metals

Aluminum foil, Aerosol cans, Bottle caps

Clothes hangers, Empty oil cans, Ferrous metal

Paint cans *(no lids; paint must be dried out)*

Non-Recyclable Plastics

#1 Microwave trays

#2 Yogurt, cottage cheese and margarine tubs,

All #3, #4, #5, #6, #7 plastics

Any bottles that held antifreeze, motor oil, bleach, pesticides, or any other hazardous material

Film canisters

Plastic bags and wrappers

Non-Recyclable Glass (Place in Trash Can)

Broken Glass

Ceramic mugs and plates

Windshield glass

Window glass

Mirrors

Light bulbs

Fluorescent tubes (broken place in a sealed plastic bag)

Recycling

Hundreds of computer drop-off programs are now being operated across the country by governments, non-profit groups, retailers, manufacturers and recyclers. In some cases a fee may be charged. The Electronics Alliance, an industry group, offers a state-by-state list on (www.eiae.org).

Recycle for beauty. Leave this world a little cleaner than you found it.

A few cities pick up electronic trash curbside. Others provide referrals to recyclers. Call your solid waste disposal department for a list of recyclers, retailers and charities that accept "e-waste" or trade-ins.

Junk is something you keep for years and then throw out two weeks before you need it.
-Source unknown-

All major computer manufacturers now "take back" obsolete computers, however the shipping costs tend to be prohibitive unless you can find a free local pickup site.

The companies then either donate working equipment or recycle the components and recover the glass, plastic, metal and circuit boards.

Contacts for the various companies are:

Compaq: 1 (888) 576-3818
Gateway: 1 (800) GATEWAY
Hewlett Packard: www.hp.com/go/recycle
IBM 1 (888) SHOP-IBM
Sony: All Sony brand electronics and personal computer equipment can be recycled free at any Waste Management, Inc. site.

General Recycling Rules

In order for recycling to work, items recycled must be clean. Rinse bottles and cans and remove bottle caps and lids.

Chapter Twenty-Four

PETS

Dogs

Beloved pets may be some of the hardest things to part with and find homes for, particularly older animals. Dearly loved pets are also the things which keep many seniors alive, since they fear what may happen to their precious companions when they are gone.

Helping them find a good home for those pets may be one of the greatest gifts you can give an older person, because it will give them peace of mind.

Complicating the problem is the fact that frequently the pets are as old and crippled as their owners.

The best place to start is to look with friends or relatives who already know the pet, and it knows them. The key question is, do they love the animal?

Next look for another person similar to the person giving up the pet. Remember there is the flip side of the problem, and that is the grieving older people who have lost their own precious pet and are pining away at the loss. Some dogs have the patience of Job, and display an innate forbearance and tolerance toward older people and can accept a similar new master easily.

Another way to find a home for a pet is to call several local veterinarians and see what suggestions they might have. Some have bulletin boards in their offices where notes and photos can be posted. Others may know of people who have lost pets and may be looking for replacements (but don't want to start off with a frisky puppy, kitten, or younger animal). Remember, veterinarians are particularly compassionate toward animals. That's why they went into the "critter" business.

> Dogs are not our whole life, but they make out lives whole.
> -Roger Caras-

One national organization that is devoted to these very needs in LOA, Little Orphan Angels. They want to help individuals who can no longer care for their pets' needs. They can be reached through the Internet at (www.littleorphanangels.org/)

Little Orphan Angels also needs pet crates, pet carriers, collars, food, bedding, nursing bottles, formula, medications, vaccinations and syringes.

No matter how much cats fight, there always seem to be plenty kittens -Abraham Lincoln (1809-1865)

An Internet site that lists names of many animal organizations that helps find new homes for pets is PetFinder.com You can type in your zip code and it will give a list of all nearby organizations. They work with both large and small animals: dogs, cats, horses, rabbits, snakes and reptiles.

If that still doesn't work, it might also pay to run an ad or post a notice on local feed store bulletin boards. It might read as follows:

"Ajax (a Black Lab) needs a loving home. He has been my faithful and intelligent companion for 16 years, but I can no longer care for him. He barks to alert me when anyone steps on the porch, and when the telephone rings. He has also alerted me to smoke when a pan caught fire. If you can use his special talents and give him a good home, please call my niece at (804) 555-8802."

One couple, planning on selling their home and moving to a retirement home, couldn't find a home for their dog no matter how they tried. Their real estate agent came up with a brilliant suggestion. The dog was included on the listing agreement, and had to be part of the deal in buying the house. It was the perfect solution. The people who bought the house loved the dog, the old owners were then free to move on, and the dog got to stay around his old haunts and buddies.

To make the transition smoother, remember to give the new owner the pet's toys, basket and blanket and supply of their favorite food. Be sure to make a list of the pet's medical history, idiosyncrasies, favorite things, likes and dislikes, etc. Be sure to include the name, address and phone number of the pet's vet.

Cats

Cats may be harder to place, not because no one will take them, but because it's the cat that decides who *it* will accept. To add to the problem, they get even more set in their ways the older they get, and it may take a long time and a lot of patience to try to get a cat to accept a new owner.

It's because of concern that no one will care for their cat that people occasionally leave their home and everything they own to Fluffy or Muffy. Perhaps the best hope of finding a new home for an old cat is to look for a similar owner. (i.e., bedridden, wheelchair bound, etc.). Indoor cats transfer more easily than more independent outdoor cats.

Some retirement centers allow new residents to bring their cats with them and keep them until the pet dies, but then not replace it.

Birds and Fish

Birds can carry diseases, so they shouldn't be placed around children who might be sickly. However if the birds are exotics, they might bring enjoyment to many if donated to your local zoo, or a school that has a small aviary.

Tropical fish, on the other hand, might be ideal "companions" for an invalid child or adult, provided there is a responsible caregiver who is willing to clean the tank regularly and see that the fish are fed.

Birds and fish might also be appreciated by group homes, schools, or senior centers. Be sure to donate the cages and the tanks too.

'Carpe Diem' does not mean 'fish of the day'.
-Unknown-

Farm Animals Large and Small

Many drug and alcohol rehabilitation ministries operate farms. So do many homes for troubled and abused youth. Caring for an animal teaches responsibility, and many a young person has learned valuable lessons riding a horse, milking a cow, brushing a llama, or gathering eggs.

There are also scores of 4-H youngsters who would jump at the chance to acquire an animal or two. They're prime candidates to give a good home to your pigs, goats, sheep, ducks, and geese.

Horses

The same groups that take farm animals would also be ideal candidates for donations of horses. However, horses also fall into a separate category because of their versatility, and there are groups that definitely are in need of horses.

Some of the above mentioned "youth ranches" take their young charges out on actual cattle round-ups and to do range work or trail rides. Then there are youth camps and church camps with equestrian programs, and also some wonderful horse programs for handicapped and inner city kids. Start by checking with your local riding stable. If donating horses, donate the saddle and tack and any leftover feed too if possible.

Exotic Animals

Does your local zoo or wildlife farm accept donations? If not, try the 4-H kids again, or call several local vets and ask if they know anyone who would give a home to a pot bellied pig, snake, ferret, emu, llama or what have you. You might also check with juvenile offender rehabilitation ranches and drug and rehabilitation farms.

Pet Food

Love the animals: Our Father has made them and wondrous they are!

Most humane societies and many senior centers collect pet food for low-income pet owners. In the Seattle area, for instance, the Humane Society needs to collect almost 6 tons of pet food every month.

Many seniors and people living with confining diseases face economic and emotional hardships, and their pets may be their only source of companionship, joy, exercise or a daily routine.

Contact your local Humane Society or Senior Center if you have pet food to donate.

Cages, Pens, Fencing & Horse Trailers

Many of the residential youth ranches that take in young people who have had brushes with the law have found that pairing the youth with animals has a very therapeutic effect. Many a tough street kid has softened when given the responsibility to feed a bunny, chicken or goat. The same is true of the farm programs that get drug and alcohol abusers back in touch with the land and with nature. Such operations can always use "critter containers," — cages, pens, trailers and feed, — *LOTS* of feed!

There's no need to fear the wind if your haystacks are tied down.
-Irish Proverb-

How to Dispose of your Stuff

Chapter Twenty-Five

GIVING OF YOURSELF

Your Medical History

One of the greatest things you can leave for future descendants is a "health profile" which may provide clues to genetic traits and health problems that may be inherent to you and your family. Particularly as people start to age and health issues begin to show up, doctors invariably ask "is this in your family?" All too frequently, people have no idea.

Write a little synopsis about yourself telling important things such as blood type, (*always* list that) eye color, hair color, height, weight and shape, (such as, "I'm 6' tall, big boned and stocky. My mother and all my aunts were also over 6' tall and on the heavy side. I had one uncle who was 6' 6 and weighed 300 lbs, but was so strong he could lift a cow.") That type of information may solve a mystery in two or three generations to a bunch of 6' tall, strong people who have no idea who or which side of the family gave them their "tall" and "strong" genes.

Next tell *your own* health history: what childhood diseases you had, then what adult diseases. Note any adult "inherited" problems such as gallstones, kidney stones, high blood pressure, heart disease or diabetes. How's your eyesight? Are you nearsighted or farsighted? Do you wear glasses? What's your shoe size? Do you have flat feet or bone spurs?

What old age problems are you running into? Is there any history of arthritis, osteoporosis, stroke, diverticulitis, female or prostate problems? What surgery have you had? Are there any allergies or predispositions to certain things (broken bones, "every cold that comes along," the annual flu, or whatever)?

Hair

Tell about your hair. What color was it as a child, then as an adult? Is your hair thick or thin? Is it straight or curly? At what age did you start to gray? Is there

If I had known I was going to live this long, I'd have taken better care of myself.
-Eubie Blake (at age 100)-

any baldness in the family? You might even tape a snippet of hair to your report. (Good for checking a descendant's blood line via your DNA in years to come.)

Ways to Collect DNA Samples

Another way to collect a DNA sample has been developed by the KlaasKids Foundation and the State of California DNA Laboratory. They have created a Do-It-Yourself DNA Collection system using common household items. With it, you can sample and store your DNA with total confidence, but without the unnecessary expense of purchasing DNA kits that can cost between $5.00 and $20.00 each.

DNA analysis if fast becoming the "genetic fingerprint" of the new millennium. Simply put, DNA is the fundamental building block that defines us an individuals. Each cell of every living entity contains DNA that is unique to that person, animal or plant. Your DNA is exactly the same in every one of your cells and nobody else's DNA is exactly like yours.

The necessary equipment is: one cotton swab, two zip-lock plastic bags (you can also use sterile gauze or a clean piece of filter paper).

The procedure is to rub a clean (sterile if possible) cotton swab, sterile gauze or filter paper) on the inside of the cheek until moist. Let the specimen air dry for twenty-four hours. When dry, place it in a zip-lock bag and seal the bag. Label the bag with permanent pen, noting the person's name and sample date. Save it in the freezer until if or whenever needed. Follow the same procedure for a blood sample. (However wait until the donor scrapes or cuts him or herself before taking the sample.) You may also save baby teeth and nail clippings in the same manner. All yield valuable DNA.

Hereditary Family Health

Next tell everything you know about other known health problems *in your family*. Think about your parent's health, and that of your brothers and sisters and your children. (Those are your "first-degree relatives.") Just writing it all down may start to show a pattern of things to watch for, or things that may be passed on to descendants.

Next add any information you know about "second-degree relatives," - grandparents, cousins, aunts and uncles. If there are known genetic problems in your family, note at what age they became apparent in various members. If the family members are deceased, note their cause of death and age at which they died.

Add any stray comments that may amplify or give additional information, such as: ("people always knew it was a Jones kid by their freckles" or "every one of us kids had identical hands with exceptionally long and very crooked fingers.")

Is there any cancer in the family? How about things like manic depression, alcohol abuse, birth defects, multiple sclerosis, kidney disease or bone problems? Even noting little things, such as "prone to nose bleeds" or "has no sense of smell" is very important information.

Finally, list everything, even if it's just one liners, or family "tales" *about ancestors*. An ancient aunt had "shaking palsy," or an uncle had "strangury." Reading through your family genealogy may show ailments unknown to us by their archaic names. These are precious bits of information, so note them again in the document you are producing.

Leave his document in your strongbox or safe deposit box, or put it in the care of the family genealogist, and suggest that each family member prepare a similar health profile.

Just for the record, if some ancestor left a similar document, but you don't know what the old ailments are, here's a present day translation: "Strangury" is difficulty urinating, rheumatism was "screws," Chronic colitis was "old soldier's disease," "camp fever," Jail fever or "ship's fever" is typhus.

"Shaking palsy" is Parkinson's Disease. "Green sickness" or "falling disease" is Epilepsy. "Membranous croup" is Diphtheria. "Pertussis" is Whooping Cough.

Methuselah lived to be 969 Years old. You boys and girls will see more in the next fifty years than Methuselah saw in his whole lifetime.
-Mark Twain-

A cold was "coryza" and an infection was "corruption." Tuberculosis was "lung sickness." Diphtheria was "putrid fever," tonsillitis was "quinsy and infant diarrhea caused by spoiled milk was called "summer complaint."

Insanity was "mania," Osteomyelitis was "hip gout," epilepsy was "falling sickness," rupture of a blood vessel was "extravasted blood," laryngitis was "aphonia," "hydrophobia was K-9 madness," iron deficiency anemia was "chlorosis."

God doesn't give people talents that He doesn't want people to use.
-Iron Eagle-

Constipation was "costiveness," edema swelling (sometimes by kidney or heart disease) was "dropsy," and acid indigestion was "dyspepsia." Scrofula was "king's evil," pneumonia was "lung fever" and malaria was "remitting fever."

Inherited Talents

Finally, note what common talents are inherent in the family. Do you come from a long line of carpenters? farmers? great cooks or bakers? writers? artists? Does playing a musical instrument "come naturally" to those in your clan, or is singing as normal as talking?

The fact is, you are just one person in a long line of people in your family, and this little gold mine of health information you are compiling may well be the most valuable thing you leave those who will come after you. It may even help save a life or two, by giving descendants fair warning of things to watch for and catch early (in the case of hereditary physical afflictions) or what talents to look for and cultivate.

Everyone is born with at least one talent, and most have several. Encourage those who carry on the family bloodline to discover their talent, develop it, and if possible, figure out how to make a living at it. One of the keys to real happiness is being able to make the most of doing what you love.

If you see young people in the family showing early signs of true talent, encourage and nurture them. Your small efforts may pay big dividends in helping them develop and happy and satisfying life.

Your Memoirs or Autobiography

There's an old saying that when an old person dies, it's as though some great library burned to the ground. We spend our lifetime accumulating a wealth of wisdom and knowledge, and what is to become of that?

While we're disposing of "stuff", the "stuff" in our heads (our knowledge and memories) is as important (or more so) than any material goods we may leave. Anyone who has ever seen their family genealogy knows how sparse personal information is about those who came before us. The only thing we know about some people is two or three words, such as "died in childbirth", "big ears" or "horse thief." What will be told about us? The best way to leave an accurate synopsis of your life is to write it yourself.

You're not a writer? Then make an oral history. Talk into a tape recorder about special moments in your life, and about experiences with everyone else in your family. Were you in the military or go through the Great Depression? Tell about it. Drop lots of names of relatives and tell how you're related. (Future family genealogists will thank you for it!)

Talk about your spouse, and about each of your children in turn. Throw in a few funny stories like the time the kids were snooping for Christmas presents and knocked over the Christmas tree, or the time little Martha got so mad she sat down and ate grass.

Young people find it hard to imagine life without television and computers. Tell memories from your childhood. Did you ever ride in a rumble seat? Did your mom cook on a wood stove? Did the old homestead have indoor plumbing when you were a kid? Did you ride a school bus or walk to school? Tell about your clothespin dolls and how you made ballerinas from hollyhocks.

**History will be kind to me, for I intend to write it.
-Sir Winston Churchhil-**

Forget worrying about sounding like Methuselah's grandma and tell it like it really was. We'll guarantee that such a tape will become a cherished family heirloom. The grandchildren will marvel and look at you as really having had a deprived childhood without TV. But the fact is, you have a chance to teach that you witnessed and were a part of America's history, and they will be too. And when you're finished making this tape, don't forget to pop the little tabs on the cartridge to prevent accidentally recording over the original.

Happy is the man who knows what to remember of the past, what to enjoy in the present, and what to plan for in the future.
-A. Gibson-

Are you a Veteran or ex-War Worker?

If you were, Uncle Sam wants your memories! There are 19 million war veterans living in the United States today. But every day we lose 1,500 of them. Motivated by the urgent need to collect the stories and experiences of war veterans while they are still living, the United States Congress created the Veteran's History Project.

This massive undertaking is an effort to gather the recollections of anyone who served in the military in any war, (World War I, World War II, the Korean, Vietnam and Persian Gulf Wars) or worked in the war-related industries. (Examples of the latter include building planes, tanks, ships or weapons, civilians working on military bases, as instructors, inspectors, defense workers, Civil Air Patrol, USP or Red Cross workers.)

The Project wants one recording not to exceed 90 minutes for each veteran. Upon completion, your recording will be housed permanently in the Library of Congress American Folklife Center or local archives that are participating partners of the Veterans History Project at the Library of Congress. Do not send any tapes or transcripts without the necessary accompanying forms and releases.

You can get a free project kit with lots of helpful forms and instructions for recording and registering your oral history by calling or writing:

The Veterans History Project
American Folklife Center
Library of Congress
101 Independence Avenue SE
Washington, DC 20540-4615

Veterans History Project
Phone: (202) 707-4916
Message Line: 1-888-371-5848
FAX: (202) 252-2046
Email: vohp@loc.gov
Web site URL: http:www.loc.gov/folklife/vets

Your Military Records

You may think your 50-year old military records aren't important anymore. The fact is, they are, and regardless of how old you are, you still need them. What for? Your family genealogy, for one thing.

They're also important if you want to be buried in a National Cemetery, or if you want a military headstone, for another. Regardless of your age, if you are a veteran, gather these records NOW and keep them with your most valuable papers.

It takes a while to replace lost records, so here's how you do it if you don't have yours. You must send a completed Form SF180 to:

The National Personnel Records Center
Military Personnel Records
9700 Page Avenue
St. Louis, MO 63132-5100

There was a disastrous fire July 12, 1973, when 16 to 18 million military personnel files were destroyed. 80% of Army records for personnel discharged between November 1, 1912 to January 1, 1960 were lost, as were 75% of Air Force records for personnel discharged between September 25, 1947 to January 1, 1964.

No duplicate copies of the records that were destroyed in the fire were maintained, nor was a microfilm copy ever produced. There were no indexes created prior to the fire.

**Be Prepared
-Boy Scout Motto-**

Therefore, a complete listing of the records that were lost is not available. Nevertheless, NPRC (MPR) uses many alternate sources in its efforts to reconstruct basic service information to respond to requests, so don't give up hope. The NPRC will do everything possible to reconstruct your records.

To Request Your Records

Form SF180 is available on-line at:
www.nara.gov/regional/mprsf180.html

If you don't have access to a printer, you may request it via fax from the National Archives and Records Administration Fax-on-Demand system. The SF180 is available as Document 2255. The Fax-on-Demand phone number is (301) 713-6905. You must have a fax machine to print the response. (You can do all this via a computer or FAX at your local Kinko's too.)

You could also send your request by mail. Requests must contain enough information to identify your record from among the more than 70 million on file at NPRC. The information they will need is the veteran's complete name used while in the service, service number or social security number, and the date and place of birth. If the request pertains to a record that may have been involved in the 1973 fire, also include place of discharge, last unit of assignment, and place of entry into the service if known.

Turnaround times for records requested from the National Personnel Records Center (NPRC) vary greatly depending on the nature of the request. For example, the NPRC Military Records Facility currently has a backlog of over 200,000 requests and receives approximately 5,000 requests daily. Routine requests for separation statements currently require 4-5 weeks for servicing. The average turnaround time for all requests is currently 14-16 weeks; however requests that involve reconstruction efforts due to the 1973 fire may take much longer.

Military medals and awards and Cold War Recognition Certificates are also replaceable at no charge.

To Request Burial in a Military Cemetery or Headstone

Gravesites in national cemeteries cannot be reserved in advance; they can only be applied for once the veteran has died. Reservations made prior

A family is a place where principles are hammered and honed on the anvil of everyday living.
-Charles Swindoll-

to 1962 will be honored, however. Families are encouraged to prepare in advance by discussing cemetery options, collecting the veteran's military information including discharge papers, and by contacting the cemetery where burial is desired.

For burial in a private cemetery: If the veteran's burial will be in a private cemetery and a Government headstone or marker will be requested for the veteran's grave, that family must complete VA Form 40-1330 (Application for Standard Government Headstone or Marker for Installation in a Private or State Veterans' Cemetery) in advance, and place it with the veterans military discharge papers for use at the time of need.

To Request A Bugler to Play Taps

As mentioned on page 234, Bugles Across America attempts to supply a live bugler to play "Taps" at the funeral of as many veterans as possible. Check on their website (www.buglesacrossamerica.org/) to see if they have volunteers in your area, or check with your local veteran's organizations.

Leave a Photo Heritage Too

Take lots of pictures. Don't disappear off the face of the earth without leaving behind a good picture of your face. "Nobody would want it," you may be thinking, but that isn't true. If you're known in your community, your local newspaper should already have (or would appreciate) a photo of you in their photo morgue.

Even more important, you should be leaving photos of yourself for your descendents. Those familiar with genealogy can tell you the thrill of going through family photos and seeing "the family nose" or "the beauty spot" or whatever, showing up again and again. Perhaps some future child who may be named after you would love to see a photo of his or her namesake.

Videotape yourself telling family stories too. You can never leave too many tidbits of information or photos.

All good men must die, but death cannot kill their names.
-Spanish Proverb-

Your Words of Wisdom

Just as you can give your family their past by giving them their genealogy, you can also give them guidance for their future. Within the Jewish faith, parents have long been encouraged to write "wills" in which they pass down life's lessons to their spiritual heirs.

Train up a child in the way he should go, and when he is old, he will not depart from it.
-Proverbs 22:6-

What particular credos or principles do you live by and that you would like to see carried on by your descendants? Write a "What I Believe" letter to those who follow you, with perhaps a personal note attached to each young recipient. Subjects you might expound on are your morals, integrity, patriotism, and your faith.

Touch on the value of a good reputation, being a man or woman of your word, acts of kindness that have been done for you, and that you have done for others.

The Spiritual Inheritance You Pass On

Of all the things you pass on to future generations, nothing is more important than your faith. Earthly goods are dross compared with sharing your belief in Eternal Life in Christ with your descendents. This is not optional. 1 Peter 1:4 admonishes us to pass on this most important of all inheritances. It tells us this is the one thing that can never perish, spoil or fade, and that it is kept in heaven for you and yours.

Expound on your faith. Write down how you came to the Lord, and talk about your personal life with Christ and what HE means to you. Stress to your children and grandchildren the importance of marrying godly men and women.

Either send these "spiritual wills" out now, or leave them in an addressed envelope in your strongbox or safe deposit box.

Chapter Twenty-Six

LIFE GIVING DONATIONS

Just as giving blood to the Red Cross Blood Bank allows us to give life to others without diminishing our own, there are other things we can donate while alive that either give life, or a better quality of life to others. The bible tells us in Leviticus 17:11 "The life is in the blood" so blood truly is the gift of life.

Do you have a great deal of weight to lose and are you contemplating stomach stapling? We heard of one lady who lost over 300 pounds and had plastic surgery to get rid of rolls of extra skin. That skin was worth its weight in gold to the skin bank for use on burn victims. If you have the same potential skin donation, you might even find there's someone out there willing to pay for your plastic surgery.

Donated Hair

Numbers 6:19 tells us that hair is another item defined in the bible as a sacrifice. This is one more of those things that are a minor contribution on the part of the giver, but major on the part of the recipient. Not many women wear long hair these days, but many do have old braids or ponytails from their childhood tucked away in their dressers or hope chests.

Your descendents may not want your tresses, but many hair-loss victims do. Locks of Love is a non-profit organization that provides hairpieces to financially disadvantaged children across the U.S. suffering from long-term medical hair loss. Most of the children helped by LOL have lost their hair due to a medical condition called alopecia areata that has no known cause or cure.

> But if a woman has long hair, it is a glory to her. For her hair is given to her for a covering.
> 1 Corinthians 11:15

The prostheses LOL provides helps restore the children's sel-esteem and confidence, enabling them to more comfortably face the world and their peers. They need hair at least 10" long (tip to tip), no wigs, falls or synthetic hair. (You may pull curly hair straight to measure the minimum 10".)

The clean, dry hair should be in a ponytail or braid and placed in a plastic bag. They need hair from both men and women, young and old, all colors and from all races. The hair may be colored or "permed," but not chemically damaged (if you're not sure, ask your stylist).

Hair cut years ago is useable as long as it has been stored in a ponytail or braids. Hair that is short, gray, or unsuitable for children will be separated from the ponytails and sold at fair market value to offset the cost of manufacturing. Layered hair may be put into more than one ponytail for donation. Hair swept off the floor is not useable.

Many hair stylists and salons will cut your hair free if you are donating it to Locks of Love. (Contact them or check out their website (www.locksoflove.com) for a salon in your city.

Locks of Love
1640 S. Congress Ave., Suite 104
Palm Springs, FL 33461
Phone: (561) 963-1677; FAX (561) 963-9914
Toll Free Info Line: 1-(888) 896-1588

Wigs for Kids is a not-for-profit organization providing hair replacement solutions for children affected by hair loss due to chemotherapy, alopecia, burns and other medical conditions. Their objective is to help children look themselves by alleviating additional stress due to lack of understanding among their peers.

The primary difference between Wigs for Kids and Locks of Love is that Wigs for Kids requires the donation to be 12" in length, and Locks of Love will take hair 10" long.

Wigs for Kids, Executive Club Building
213330 Center Ridge Road, Suite C
Rocky River, OH 44116
Phone: (440) 333-4433, FAX (440) 333-0200
Email: info@wigsforkids.org
Website: (www.wigsforkids.org)

How beautiful you are. Your eyes are like doves behind your veil; your hair is like a flock of goats that have descended from Mt. Gilead.
Song of Solomon 4:1

Giving of Your Time and Talents Here and Now

President Bush has called upon every American to donate two years of volunteer service to others, but this doesn't mean you have to show up at a recruiting office to sign up.

We are all surrounded by hundreds of needs and opportunities. A few minutes of our time and talent might make a major difference in a lonely life. It doesn't require someone to be hale and hearty to teach a child to read. A patient bed-ridden grandma could do it.

Volunteers are not paid, not because they are worthless, but because they are priceless.

Likewise with helping a struggling child with homework, or teaching valuable life-skills to a child with no good role models in his or her home. Sometimes even the lowliest of jobs can be the most rewarding.

Have you ever thought of the church janitor, keeping God's house clean? That's one place where you'll never be alone! What about volunteering at a local hospital for a few hours of just rocking and loving a baby born to a mother on drugs? Or give Salvation Army a helping hand at Christmas time as a bell ringer?

Yes, there are some volunteer jobs that require specialized skills, like being able to enter data into a computer program, or doing the wiring for a Habitat for Humanity house, but for every job that requires a skill, there are dozens that don't. How about simply making phone calls to shut-ins, or elderly friends, just to make sure they're all right?

Or how about taking your collection of Golden Oldies to a nursing home, just to give the old timers a trip down memory lane? Is there an Old Soldier's home near you? So many of our aging heroes have no family or loved ones left to listen to their old war stories. What does it matter that you don't know them, or that they forget some of the details? Maybe you could even write down their stories for the Veterans History Project (page 169).

One person can't do everything, but one person can do something.
-President George W. Bush, Feb. 10, 2003

Food Banks can always use an extra hand to help sort, bag, and hand out foods. Or perhaps you could pick up end-of-date bread milk, vegetables and meat from your neighborhood grocery stores and deliver it to the food bank. Millions of dollars worth of perfectly good food could be recovered daily and put to good use if only more people would just take on this simple task.

Can you bake cookies or serve coffee? Do you live near a big airport? Did you know the USO is still in business, and has lounges run by volunteers for traveling service men and women?

Lots of organizations need drivers. Drivers are always needed to take elderly people to medical appointments, grocery shopping or to church. Do you drive to a distant town or certain place each week? Perhaps you could offer a ride to a senior who has a loved one in that town, or drop them off with a doctor or to shop while you conduct your business.

Many seniors or handicapped people need a helping hand with household chores, cooking or shopping. What may be simple tasks for us may be monumental hurdles for them. There are many kind Samaritans who have their own crosses to bear, who can do nothing more than read the bible to an AIDS sufferer in their final days.

Chapter Twenty-Seven

The Ultimate Arrangements

Another of the great gifts we can leave our loved ones, is good detailed instructions of what care we wish for ourselves as we get older and face the possibility of not being able to care for ourselves. By making these plans ourselves we can ease the burden of decision-making that could fall upon members of the family.

Also, by beginning to think about possible situations and options before a crisis, you will have time to gather information and make more informed and thoughtful decisions. You may find it helpful to talk options over with friends, family members, your clergyman, your doctor, and your attorney.

Health Care

Everyone is entitled to make the decisions about their health care and the right to accept or refuse care. Modern medicine can often prolong life of the terminally ill or severely incapacitated even though the patient has no hope of recovery. Many people have no desire to prolong life in such a condition, while others want every available form of treatment tried in order to be kept alive as long as possible.

When patients are unable to understand information about proposed treatment and make reasoned decisions, they are considered to be incapacitated. Thus it is essential to clarify your thoughts and feelings and draw up your preferences while you can still do your planning for yourself.

Advance Directives

Instructions should cover the following areas and you should leave written directions as to:

1. **Caregiver**: Is there a special relative, caregiver, nurse, home care organization, or nursing home we wish to have care for us, *or not care for us* should we become incapacitated? If possible, also name a substitute caregiver.

Even if you make a mistake in decisions regarding disposal of your estate, it won't be as bad as not making any decisions at all.

Where there's a will, there's a way

2. **Keys**: Arrange for a trusted neighbor, relative, friend or building superintendent to have a set of instructions in case of emergency.

3. **Current Health Data**: The name of your physician(s), preferred hospital or HMO, list of medications (note the dosages and times they should be taken), and name and phone number of an emergency contact. Be sure your doctor's office has the current names and numbers of your emergency contacts on file. Also be sure your doctor's office has the name and phone number of another contact besides yourself.

4. **Advance Directives** for emergency contingencies: Leave clear instructions stating your wishes for medical care should you become incapable of making the decision. Leave a signed "Advanced Directives" form, Durable Power of Attorney for Healthcare, or Living Will with your spouse or most trusted relative, and physician or health care provider. You should discuss your decisions in detail with your family and friends, your physician and attorney, so that those who may be called upon to make decisions on your behalf are fully aware of your wishes.

You can also obtain a bracelet that indicates you don't want CPR performed in the event of a cardiac or respiratory arrest. To obtain a bracelet, you must fill out a No-CPR directive, which will be kept on file with your health care provider, and must be posted in a visible place in your home.

5. **Financial matters**: In case someone has to (or may have to) take over your financial matters, make a detailed list of all insurance policies, both life and health insurance, including policy numbers, agent's names, and names and addresses of the companies. You should also have a current list of all assets, including property (in and out of state), stocks, bonds, savings accounts and other investments. Your spouse and your attorney should have copies of this list. History abounds with sad tales of widows and families whose loved ones never left them such a list, and in many instances, their inheritance went unclaimed.

Put one copy in your safe deposit box, strongbox or safe, and give another copy to your lawyer to keep in your client file.

6. **The Living Will**: What are your wishes for life support and final care in the event you come down with a terminal illness or go into a coma? The Living Will is a directive to doctors and families declaring a person's decision to refuse life-sustaining medical treatment in the event of terminal illness or injury or becoming permanently unconscious. Even though the directive allows your doctor to withhold or withdraw life-sustaining treatment, comfort care will continue to be provided. The Living Will does not authorize "mercy killing" or any procedure that would actually speed up the natural process of dying.

The Living Will must be signed in the presence of two qualified witnesses. The following persons may *not* serve as witnesses: anyone related to you by blood or marriage, anyone entitled to part of your estate by will or otherwise, anyone with a claim against your estate, your doctor, or any employee or volunteer of your health care provider.

7. **The Durable Power of Attorney**: Many people use a Durable Power of Attorney for Healthcare instead of, or in addition to, a Living Will. Compared to the Living Will, a Durable Power of Attorney may allow you to more fully express your wishes concerning care. It is also more broadly applicable since it can apply to nearly any type or level of healthcare during periods of incapacitation. Although many Senior Resource Centers provide Durable Power of Attorney forms, you may wish to consult with your own attorney to help assure that your document clearly states your wishes and is consistent with applicable legal requirements. (This document can also create a dangerous situation. Remember our Christian lady in the Foreword who gave one to her sister.)

> Living Wills should be very specific about the definition of "brain dead" and not so carelessly worded that they can be enacted by greedy heirs if your foot goes to sleep.
> -P.J. O'Rourke

8. **The final disposition**: Your body. Do you have a prepaid funeral plan? Do you want to be buried or cremated, or perhaps are you considering donating your body to science? Where do you want to be bur-

ied? Do you already own a cemetery plot? What arrangements are already made? Who is to officiate at your service? Make a list of special friends and acquaintances you want notified, complete with their names, addresses and telephone numbers.

Many people even write their own obituaries, or leave notes of items they want included in the obituary. Others write their own eulogies and design their tombstones, and make complete plans for their funeral or memorial arrangements, down to choosing the music, readings, and people and items they want included.

If you wish to donate your body for research or study, make arrangements with your local medical school and be sure your physician makes note of your decision.

Make several copies of the above items (except for #4, the list of your assets), and put them multiple places where they can be easily found. You might give one copy each to your doctor and lawyer, to put in your medical file and client file. Another copy should go to the most trusted person in your life. Still another could go to your best friend.

The originals should go in a big envelope marked "OPEN ME FIRST", and put it on top of your papers in your safe deposit box, strongbox or safe. It might also pay to put a set in your nightstand drawer, since your safe may not be opened for weeks after you're gone. If decisions need to be made fast, concerning your care, this will leave a clear road map of your wishes and what you do and don't want done.

There are statutory requirements that apply if you ever change your mind and wish to cancel your Living Will or Durable Power of Attorney for Healthcare. You can do so either verbally or in writing. Tell your doctor, clinic, or hospital medical records department staff in person that you wish to cancel the directive, or sign and date a written statement indicating your wish to cancel your directive, then send copies to

> Good resolutions are like babies crying in church. They should be carried out immediately.
> -Charles M. Shelton-

everyone who needs to know. If you change your mind about donating organs and tissue, be sure to destroy your wallet card.

Taking care of the above paperwork is also the final step of "putting your affairs in order", and should give you immense satisfaction that you have done everything humanly possible to make it as easy as possible, and as little burden as possible, on those you leave behind.

Organs and Tissue

For Christians, who are awaiting the "upper-taker," not the undertaker, this should not be a hard choice. The bible tells us that we will get a new body in heaven. Thus this old earthly body can be left behind with no regrets. Even it can be "recycled" with many parts put to good use by others once we're through with it.

The only hope for many thousands of people suffering from organ failure is that a donor will make the ultimate gift of life upon his own death, -the needed organ. Today the number of Americans awaiting life-saving organs is approaching 40,000, while hundreds of thousands more could benefit from tissue transplants. Tragically, the need for donated organs and tissue continues to outpace supply.

There are two types of life-saving donations, living and non-living.

Under "living donations," a living donor in good health can donate a kidney, a portion of a liver or lung, bone marrow or blood to another person.

None-living donations are those done shortly after the time of death.

Needed organs include the heart, kidneys, pancreas, lungs, liver and intestines. Tissue that can be donated includes the eyes, corneas, skin, bone, bone marrow, heart valves and tendons. One donor can potentially help more than 50 other people live.

If organ and tissue donation is consistent with your life values and faith, there are several steps to take to assure your wishes will be respected upon your death.

The Lord was pleased to strengthen us, and remove all fear from us, and dispose our hearts to be as useful as possible.
-Richard Allen, 1760-1831-

Discuss your decision with your family and explain why you want to be a donor. It is important for your family to support your commitment. Your local Donor Program can supply you with literature that will explain the program fully and answer any questions. There is no cost to the donor's family or estate.

Fill out a Uniform Donor Card

I, _____ have spoken to my family about organ and tissue donation. The following people have witnessed my commitment to be a donor.

I wish to donate the following:
- any needed organs and tissue
- only the following organs and tissue ____

_____

Donor Signature_____Date_____
Witness_____
Witness_____

Carry your advance directives card in your billfold at all times. Review your advance directives every five years or so. Amend them if necessary, or reaffirm that they still represent your wishes.

To repeat, be sure your family knows your wishes because they WILL be consulted before donation will take place.

If The Law Decides

A single conversation with a wise man is better than ten years of study.
-Chinese Proverb-

In the event you do not leave your own Advance Directives for your care, some states have laws that define which family members and others may act as substitute decision-makers for an incapacitated patient. In Washington State, for instance, the act says that physicians must seek consent to care from people in the following classes, in the order of priority listed:

1. The appointed guardian of the patient, if any
2. The person to whom the patient has granted a Durable Power of Attorney for Healthcare
3. The patient's spouse
4. The patient's children who are at least eighteen years old
5. Parents of the patient
6. Adult brothers and sisters of the patient

The currency of this world will be worthless at our death or at Christ's return, both of which are imminent.
-Randy C. Alcorn-

Chapter Twenty-Eight

MISCELLANEOUS

Frequent Flyer Miles

Each year 50 billion unclaimed frequent-flyer miles go to waste. For just five minutes of time the "Make-A-Wish Foundation" or "Miles for Kids in Need" could put these miles to incredibly good use. These organizations fly seriously ill children off to fulfill a special wish, or to receive needed medical treatment.

Aeronautics was neither an industry nor a science. It was a miracle
-Igor Sikorsky-

To donate your miles, or for further information, contact:

Make-A-Wish Foundation of America
3550 North Central Avenue, Suite 300
Phoenix, AZ 85012-2127
1-(800) 304-9474

Make-A-Wish needs miles from America West Airlines, American Airlines, British Airways, Continental Airlines, Delta Airlines, Northwest Airlines, Southwest Airlines, United Airlines, and US Airways.

Starlight Foundation International participates in American Airlines Miles For Kids In Need Program. If you are an AAdvantage member and would like to donate excess miles to Starlight, they can put them to good use. They are also part of the Hilton Hhonors® Worldwide program. If you are an Hhonors member and would like to contribute 10,000 points as a $25 cash donation to Starlight, contact them at:

Starlight Foundation International
5900 Wilshire Boulevard, Suite 2530
Los Angeles, CA 90036
1-(800) 274-7827

Miles for Kids In Need is an American Airlines program designed to provide airfare for children in need of medical treatment, or to fulfill the wish of an ill child.

Miles For Kids In Need
P.O. Box 619616
Dallas/Fort Worth Airport, TX 75261-9616
(817) 963-8188

Real Estate and Land

Real property (land) is definitely a part of the estate and should only be disposed of after consultation with your family, your attorney and your accountant. In the event one has no heirs, or no heirs that want the property in questions, there are countless organizations that would love to have it.

A residence, vacation home, farm, acreage or vacant lot can provide tax benefits when contributed. You can frequently avoid all sizeable Capital Gains tax, remove that asset from your taxable estate, and receive a charitable deduction for the full fair market value of the property.

In addition, it is possible to make a gift of your home, farm or vacation home while retaining the right to use it for the rest of your life and that of your spouse, and receive a tax deduction at the time of the donation.

One organization that really appreciates donations of free or low cost buildable land is Habitat for Humanity. They operate a program of helping low-income people achieve ownership of their own homes through a combination of "sweat equity" (putting at least 500 hours of their own labor into building the house) and low interest loans.

Time Shares

If no one in the family wants them, check with one of your favorite ministries. They probably won't have any use for vacation property, but they could readily use the money the sale of the time-share would bring.

As any time-share owner knows, the annual cleaning and maintenance fees can be very expensive. They frequently cost more than renting a similar unit outright would be.

Savings Bonds

This is a good time to dig out all those old Savings Bonds you haven't looked at for years. Are any of them vintage War Bonds? Are you aware that Sav-

> The problem with property is that it takes so much of your time.
> -Willem de Kooning-
> 20th century Dutch-American painter

ings Bonds issued before March 1960 are no longer earning interest? There are more than $6 billion in Savings Bonds still being held that are no longer earning interest. That money would help fund a lot of struggling ministries or pay a lot of bills.

Different classifications of bonds earn varying rates of interest and for different lengths of time. Look in the upper right-hand corner of the bond to find the date of issuance. Series E Bonds issued November 1955 and earlier earn interest for 40 years, but those issued December 1965 and later earn interest for 30 years. Series HH Bonds, earn interest for only 20 years. Once they mature, the interest stops.

If the bonds are no longer bearing interest, redeem them. Otherwise inflation and taxes will eat up any interest they did earn. There's a "trap" to be aware of if redeeming bonds too. That is cashing them in at the wrong time. You can lose up to six months of interest if you redeem those that may still be bearing interest (Series EE Bonds) at any time other than exactly every six months after the bond was issued. Bondholders forfeit more than $150 million a year by cashing in bonds at the "wrong" time, (meaning other than on their 6-month anniversary dates.)

Do you think you might have other bonds, perhaps bought as gifts when you were a child, that have disappeared over the years? Lost bonds are replaceable if you can establish a valid claim. If there's a chance you might have some, the government encourages you to file a Lost Bond Claim Form (PD1048) available from most banks, and available on-line at (www-publicdebt.treas.gov)

Many people don't realize that older Savings Bonds no longer pay interest.

Remember too, when cashing in bonds, to first redeem those earning no interest, then those paying the lowest interest rates. You should also make a list of bonds that shows the issue date, series, face value, owner and beneficiary.

Chapter Twenty-Nine

HOW TO PREVENT REACCUMULATING

There are those who swear "stuff" multiplies in the dark. Others believe it expands to fill all available space. If your objective in disposing of goods was to un-clutter your life, and you have been successful in your goal of jettisoning accumulated and unused goods, you are about to enter into phase II: How to Avoid Re-cluttering.

Even if we are successful in our efforts to get rid of our own excess, there is still the matter of others cluttering our homes and our lives for us. Many adult children tend to think of the old homestead as an unpaid storage facility. Softhearted moms can soon find their attics, basements, garages, barns, sheds, spare bedrooms and closets full of the kid's castoffs and dead long-term storage. As mom gets rid of her own accumulation, others cast covetous eyes on the available space as something they can now use and fill.

Little will prevent this but a firm "no" that really means NO!" If that doesn't work, or if an emergency necessitates temporary storage of some one else's items, at least put a specific time limit on the storage. Write up an agreement with a date by which the items will be removed. When the time is up, do what a landlord would do. Give a "three strikes then you're out" notice, and after the third warning, grit your teeth, and put the stuff out on the street, or start charging regular commercial storage rates.

The excellence of a gift lies in its appropriateness, rather than its value.
-Charles Dudley Warner (1829-1900)

How to Get By With Less

Buy less. Think ahead. Reduce waste by avoiding stores that only sell in bulk, by the dozen, by the case or by the gallon. Buy just what you need. Under-estimate rather than over-estimate.

Don't buy if you can rent. If it's an item you only use every year or two, rent or borrow it. Let somebody else store it and keep it repaired.

Before buying *anything*, ask the #1 question: "Do I love it?" If the answer is no, leave it in the store.

If you haven't used something for six months, there's a good chance you never will. Put a post-it note on it with the date. If you don't use it in the next three months, get rid of it.

> Remember that not getting what you want is sometimes a wonderful stroke of luck.
> -Dalai Lama-

Remember the old World War II motto: "Use it up, wear it out, make it do, or do without." Don't buy things just because they're the latest models. Wear the old one out first.

Don't buy anything that isn't a perfect fit and isn't ideal (comfortable, flattering, well made, etc.) in every regard. Never buy or accept anything unless you have a need for it, and a place to put it where it will not be clutter.

Avoid impulse buying. When you see something you like, examine it well, and then take time to think it over. Go have a cup of coffee and decide if you really, *REALLY* want to live with that item for a long time.

Even if something is free, don't take it if you don't really want or need it.

Cut down on subscriptions. If you only read the Wednesday and Sunday papers, then only subscribe to those two days. Share a magazine subscription with a friend, or better still, read your favorite magazines at the library instead of subscribing to them. Never save an entire publication if all you want is one article. Clip, and immediately file the article only.

Stop unconscious buying. Don't go to the mall unless you need a specific item. Shop with a list to control impulse buying.

THOSE UNWANTED INTRUSIONS
Junk Mail

Junk mail is one daily influx of clutter that can be eliminated by stopping it from ever arriving in the first place. Stop unsolicited mail by writing to the following four companies and asking that your name be removed from their mailing lists. (Be sure to send each a list of all the conceivable ways you might be listed: Mrs. Fred Jones, Ms. Fred Jones, Mrs. Mary Jones, M.E. Jones, etc.)

Direct Marketing Association
Attn: Mail Preference Service
P. O. Box 9008
Farmingdale, N.Y. 11735-9008

Donnelly Marketing, Inc.
Attn: Data Base Operations
1235 North Avenue
Nevada, IA 50201-1419

MetroMail Corporation
Attn: List Maintenance
901 West Bond
Lincoln, NE 68521-3694

R. L. Polk and Company
Attn: Name Deletion File
6400 Monroe Blvd.
Taylor, MI 48180-1814

Until the flood recedes, recycle all junk mail and mail-order catalogs, preferably unread, lest you be tempted to buy more stuff.

Also remember to never throw those unsolicited credit card offers out without first tearing off the portion with your name, address and all count numbers and bar codes and burning them or shredding them. These credit applications can easily be stolen and altered and used to apply for credit in your name, once in the trash.

They say nothing is impossible – but did you ever try to get off a mailing list?

Telephone Solicitations

Few things are as irritating as unsolicited sales calls just as you've fallen asleep or sit down to dinner. Each day millions of such calls are made by telemarketers reaching out and trying to touch someone's wallet. To add insult to injury, even computers now invade our privacy. Once you answer your phone, the computer keeps your telephone line tied up for however long it takes for the canned spiel to run its course.

Telemarketers are psychic. They always know exactly the wrong time to call.

Unlike junk mail and TV advertising that at least we can discard or ignore, telephone intrusions have been responsible for many injuries as people raced for the phone, thinking the call might be important.

Many such calls are not only dangerous to your physical health, many are also dangerous to your fiscal health! When a stranger calls, you have no idea who it really is on the other end of the line asking you to send them money, or let them into your house to sell some product or service or other. Did you know that many telemarketing operations are actually run from within prisons, and done legally? Prisoners are hired as telephone solicitors under state-run work programs. The man you're giving your credit card number to may be serving time for credit card fraud.

The Federal Trade Commission will soon be getting into the act by building a national do-not-call list intended to help people block unwanted telemarketing calls.

Telemarketers would have to check the list every three months to determine who does not want to be called. Those who call listed people could be fined up to $11,000 for each violation. Consumers would be able to file complaints by phone or online to an automated system.

It will be a while until this new FCC database is in operation, so in the meantime, to stop unwanted telephone solicitations, write to:

Telephone Preference Service,
Direct Marketing Association
P. O. Box 9014
Farmingdale, N.Y. 11735-9014

Be sure you include your name, address and telephone number, including area code, and tell them you seek to "opt-put" of receiving telephone solicitation calls, and want to be removed from their marketing lists.

Suggestions for gifts

It seems as if the entire gift industry is geared toward filling our countertops, walls, closets and drawers with knickknacks, doodads, collectibles and "isn't that cutes." To paraphrase Patrick Henry, "Eternal vigilance is not only the price of liberty, is also the only way to avoid replicating clutter."

Even if you succeed in convincing your family and friends you are determined to live a simpler lifestyle, you have presented them with the new problem of how to accommodate your wishes. What are they to give when they want to give you a gift?

Tokens of affection don't have to be "stuff." Tell them you'll cherish any gift —*that comes in an envelope!* This could include all sorts of interesting possibilities. Consider some of the following:

- a ticket to the theater or a special event you would enjoy
- a ticket to your favorite sporting event
- season tickets to your local Little Theater
- a gift certificate at your favorite store or restaurant
- a grocery store gift certificate
- a pre-paid ticket or reservation for a trip
- a weekend at a lovely bed and breakfast
- a certificate for a pre-paid portrait of yourself (your descendents will someday cherish this)
- a portrait of family loved ones
- a pre-paid registration for a continuing education class you always wanted to take
- a stock certificate, a gold or silver coin, or plain old cash
- a gift certificate good for a hairstyle, makeover, back rub, or massage
- a gift of self: a home cooked dinner (the gift giver cooks, serves and washes the dishes)
- a gourmet dinner out
- a promise to do a job you need to have done
- a gift certificate or IOU for a house cleaning or errands run
- a car wash (a good gift from a young person)
- a telephone debit card or calling card
- a gasoline debit card or gift certificate

**Simplicity is the essence of happiness
-Cedric Bledsoe-**

- a tune-up for your car
- plane or train tickets, a bus pass or ride tokens
- a personalized photo calendar of your loved ones
- a homemade family video made from copied parts of home videos or old reel-to-reel movies
- a drive to a favorite site or sentimental old location
- a pocket sized personalized photo album of loved ones
- a package of lovely note cards
- homemade pressed-flower notes or stationery
- postage stamps or small bundle of post cards
- small hobby items: such as a sable brush for an artist
- packages of seeds of favorite flowers and veggies
- membership to a museum or non-profit organization
- free baby-sitting (if recipients are young parents)
- a donation to your favorite ministry, missionary or charity in your name.
- a written promise of private one-on-one time together. Perhaps an invitation to a lovely unrushed lunch or a long afternoon "date" between a mother and son or dad and daughter. Adult children are so busy these days, many older parents feel alienated or afraid they're a bother. Little could mean more to many than some uninterrupted time with their adult children. (Hint to "kids": Don't bring the cell phone!)
- a simple card or letter telling "what you mean to me," - how much the person is loved, appreciated and admired. If there is an old hurt, ask or give forgiveness. How often have you heard grieving people say they wish they had told the deceased how much they loved them, or wishing they had made up from an old disagreement?
- a promise to "phone home" at least once a month on a specific date (like the first Monday night of every month at 7:30.)

Good gifts can definitely come in envelopes.

**Reduce the complexity of life by eliminating the needless wants of life, and the labors of life reduce themselves.
-Edwin Teale-**

Those Gifts that "Don't Comply"

Not that we suggest "looking a gift horse in the mouth", or sounding ungrateful, but if you're really serious about not re-accumulating, it will take drastic measures to cut down on new incoming clutter.

No matter how firmly or kindly you pass the word on your "envelopes only, please" gift request, there will always be one or more friends or relatives who truly believe you didn't mean for that to apply to them. Sure enough, the next special occasion, here comes something big, the wrong size or color, doesn't match anything, is ugly, or will never be used. At best, it's something else you have to store or have sitting around.

Then there will be those who didn't understand your request, so there will invariably be exceptions. Young children may give some big craft project they lovingly made, and older people may give some treasure they really want you to have.

Most people will respect your wishes and enjoy the challenge of giving an appropriate envelope gift, but there's always that one person who feels they know what's best for you, regardless of your desires. What can you do?

If the situation were reversed, what would they do? You may find that the same person who disregards your wishes wouldn't hesitate to speak up if anyone disregarded theirs.

If it was an innocent misunderstanding, and the gift was given sincerely with love and generosity, graciously accept it, and use it or dispose of it, whatever you wish. However at every opportunity make little comments about how much you're enjoying your envelope gifts, and how much you appreciated them, so they'll get the hint before the next occasion. Be sure you give them envelope gifts too.

It is very difficult to reject the gift of another, for so many givers easily misunderstand the reason for the rejection.

Other ways to dispose of a "cluttering" gift include:

• take it back to the store and get cash
• re-give it away the next time you have to give gifts

- wait an appropriate time, and then at the next gift-giving occasion, give it back to the person who gave it to you. Tell them, "I know how much you love this, and I really want *you* to enjoy it. ...I insist!!"

If it isn't the gift, but the thought that counts, then let's put those thoughts in envelopes!

- Give it to a live-in institution such as a group home or home for the retarded, so it can be used either as a gift to one of them, or for one of them to give as a gift.

- Be tactful, but honest. "Gertrude I really love it, but is there any way you could get your money back? You know we're getting rid of all our stuff, and there just won't be room for this in that new little apartment."

If they put up an argument, point out that you even have to dispose of family treasures and important items because there's no room for *them*.

Chapter Thirty

RECIPIENT GROUPS AND WHAT THEY NEED

The following pages list various types of organizations and programs that can use donations of material goods as well as money.

We have tried our best to include conscientious ministries, charities and groups that are good stewards of that, which is put into their hands.

We include Christian, Jewish and secular organizations. These listings should not be considered an endorsement by the author or the publisher; rather they should be used as a starting point in finding an organization that can use your goods.

An Overview of the Types of Organizations

There are more than 1 million groups recognized by the Internal Revenue Service as nonprofits. Of these, 600,000 organizations have charitable, tax-exempt status under Section 501c3 of the IRS Code. Even this vast number still does not reflect the hundreds of thousands more small organizations with gross receipts under $5,000.00 and most religious organizations which are not required to even apply for IRS tax-exempt status.

Of those, the list of organizations that need and want gifts of goods is almost endless. Those that do fall into two basic categories: Those who meet basic human life-sustaining needs and services, and "all others." (The latter categories include such things as libraries, museums and art and cultural organizations.)

Charities are funded in numerous ways. Some raise all their own support, and others take part in collective fund-raising efforts (such as United Way). Still others accept government funding, private foundation money, and corporate funding.

The bulk of corporate donations generally go to large charities (such as arts and cultural organizations, hospitals and educational institutions). They also tend to primarily support organizations in large cities as opposed to small or rural groups.

Our objective in this book is to help those smaller groups and organizations that are the front line troops in meeting human needs, and can and do make a difference, but are ignored by most large contributors. These are the groups who would appreciate receiving financial contributions, but are equally happy to receive valuable gifts of goods and services.

We make no attempt to rate or grade them, and since many of them perform multiple services, so we simply attempt to list them according to the main thrust of each organization.

In some cases, we give addresses of specific groups, and in others, we just put forth the type of group as an idea starter for the reader. If that is the case, we suggest you search for a local group by looking the your local telephone directory, or asking your local newspaper for leads.

Inclusion in, or emission from this list does not in any way represent the endorsement or opinions of any charity's mission or purpose.

Groups we Didn't Include

We have deliberately tried to exclude organizations that accept government funding. Many tax-exempt non-profits receive a substantial portion of their funding from the government, and we don't believe the government should be in the business of funding charities with monies that have been collected as taxes. This amounts to compelling the taxpayer to make involuntary gifts.

Also not included are thousands more very worthy organizations that want only money. Our objective is to help you dispose of your goods, not your money.

Others to keep in mind that might use "stuff" but are not included here, are political groups, alumni associations, home-school groups, block watches, crime-prevention organizations, scholarship fund raisers, and other civic groups.

The Government

The government likes gifts of "stuff" too. It could be that if what you have to donate is of historical significance, and the object is of national value, the U.S. Government might be the most appropriate recipient. To find who in the federal government can use what you've got to donate, contact the Library of Congress Exchange and Gift Division, (202) 707-5000.

If the item is of value to your state, contact your state historical museum or state library. If it is of county or city interest, check with the appropriate local museum or library where it would be of most historic value.

The Thrift Store Operators, - How They Function

Most areas have several local charities that collect usable discarded goods and sell them through thrift stores. Most report that about 50% of what they collect is suitable for re-sale. The remainder (that they can't use) they recycle even further, sometimes sending it to countries where clothing is always needed. Heavy clothing goes to Eastern Europe, lighter-weight clothing goes to South America or Africa. Clothing that is totally unusable is sold for rags. Very little goes to waste.

Thrift stores today are big business. The National Association of Resale and Thrift Shops (NARTS) estimates there are over 15,000 resale shops across the country. Most are well-lit, professionally managed and attractively decorated. Many rival department stores, except for the lower prices. Merchandise comes from collection centers (bins, trailers, and kiosks) and/or house-to-house pickup or "YooHoo's" (people who call to the trucks to stop them and donate things). Some organizations, such as Goodwill, Salvation Army, and St. Vincent dePaul, do their own collections and run their own stores.

Others are commercial thrift stores that buy their merchandise from charities who run banks of telephone solicitors. Hundreds of telephone calls are made per day asking for donations, and routing pick-ups. Some charities get paid by the square foot of merchandise collected, while others get paid by the pound. Some charities which do not run their own stores, unfortunately, get as little as 10 cents on the dollar of the sale price on items sold.

Most thrift store merchandise sells within three weeks of the time it is put on the floor. At that point the price is usually dropped and eventually about half of it finally sells. Of that which doesn't sell, most is then sorted and sold as components - metal, plastic or fabric. Clothes that don't sell are baled to be sold to third world countries or to a rag merchant.

Salvation Army

It was the Salvation Army, in 1897, which developed the concept of providing employment by salvaging items for charity. In an effort to "put idle hands to work," they collected and sorted articles that were then sold to wholesale rag and scrap dealers.

Following World War I, Stella Ellison, the wife of Orlo Ellison, one of two Montana brothers who were Salvation Army officers, came up with the idea of selling used goods to needy families. She coined the term "thrift store" and the Salvation Army thereupon became the founder of all thrift stores.

Salvation Army USA (National Headquarters)
120-130 W. 14th St.
New York, NY 10011

Salvation Army performs many ministries and public services. It runs shelters, schools, food pantries, medical clinics and feeding programs.

In addition to the items they collect for resale in their stores, they can always use linens, blankets (single bed), foods for their feeding programs, hats and mittens, coats, sweatpants and sweatshirts, personal-care items, backpacks, bags with zippers, diapers (large and extra-large really appreciated) baby food, formula, non-violent videos, socks, socks, and more socks, and games for their various services. In fact, one of their many ministries can use just about anything you have to give.

Peter Drucker of the esteemed Peter F. Drucker Foundation for Nonprofit Management has called the Army the "most effective organization in the United States." Drucker adds, "No one even comes close to it with respect to clarity of mission, ability to innovate, measurable results, dedication and putting money to maximum use." To which we say, Amen!

Consider this: The Salvation Army pays its top executive, John Busby, just $13,000 a year, plus frugal room, board and transportation expenses. The Army officers follow Mr. Busby's lead, and work long hard hours for little material reward. His philosophy, which is reflected by the entire organization, is "I don't miss anything you can buy with money. I'm in the will of God, doing what He wants me to do. There's no higher purpose than that."

Goodwill Industries

Beginning in 1902, a Boston Methodist minister, Rev. Edgar Helms collected used household goods and clothing in wealthier areas of the city, then trained and hired poor people and immigrants to mend and repair these goods. The items were then resold or given to the people who repaired them. The system worked, and the Goodwill philosophy of "a hand up, not a handout" was born.

Dr. Helms' vision set an early course for what would one day become a $1.5 billion nonprofit organization. He described Goodwill Industries as both an "industrial program as well as a social service enterprise, — a provider of employment, training and rehabilitation for people of limited employability, and a source of temporary assistance for individuals whose resources were depleted."

Goodwill is the world's largest nonprofit provider of employment and training services for people with disabilities and other disadvantageous conditions, such as welfare dependency, illiteracy, criminal history and homelessness.

Goodwill Industries, International
9200 Wisconsin Avenue
Bethesda, MD 20814-3896
(301) 530-6500

Missionaries

It's always wonderful to get a package from home, and it must be particularly so for missionaries abroad, most of whom live such a sparse existence to begin with. Keep in mind when giving goods to missionaries, to include some items that they might enjoy personally, or be able to use in their ministry.

We once heard of some missionaries telling of opening a package from a lady in their home church, to find the lady had carefully dried, packaged up and shipped them all her used tea bags. The poor couple didn't know whether to laugh or cry! Others have told of getting used toothbrushes!

Suggestions for things to include in packages to missionaries would include some nice soft toilet paper and Kleenex, Band-Aides, cold medicine, aspirin, candy, and popcorn. (Missionaries like care packages packed with popcorn seeds.) Illustrated children's storybooks would be good too (because the pictures might be worth the proverbial thousand words when ministering to children.)

Ministries

There's a ministry for every conceivable need, and many of them are listed on these pages.

Many churches have needs too, and just as individuals have stuff to dispose of, so do churches. While some churches upgrade and get new hymnals and choir robes, there are other struggling congregations with no hymnals or robes. To help get the two together, there's a wonderful Internet on-line swap meet for churches at www.rca.org/resources/

swapread.html where "needs" and "wants" are posted. A typical sampling of items needed includes hymnals, choir robes, risers, pianos, organs, instruments, Christian books, communion trays and glasses, offering boxes, pulpits, vans and busses. Most recipients are willing to pay shipping or postage.

Abused and Neglected Children

Young children who have been through traumatic experiences need "escape" type things like, children's books, clean funny videos, writing and drawing paper, crayons, paints and brushes, arts and crafts supplies, Play-Doh®, puppets, a dollhouse and furniture, Legos® child-size furniture, musical instruments, school supplies, rain coats, sweatshirts and little treasures of their own, like a wrist watch, pretty hair ribbons or a little locket.

Abused Women's Shelters

Abused and battered women and their children frequently arrive at domestic abuse shelters with little more than the shirts on their backs. Their immediate needs are usually the most basic of necessities (clothing, food, shelter).

These shelters can also use alarm clocks, art materials (such as flannel board, puppets, markers, butcher paper, etc.) baby walkers, strollers, buggies, baby clothes, backpacks (school packs), basketballs, bath products (oils, beads, foams, and liquid soaps), batteries (especially D and AA), beadwork kits, bus tokens, pocket-size calendars for residents, children's bicycles and tricycles (all sizes), child-size tables and chairs, clothing (women's and children's), combs, hair brushes, cosmetics, cribs, crib sheets, baby blankets, curling irons, diapers and wipes, doll houses with furniture and dollhouse dolls and easels.

They also want personal hygiene and feminine hygiene products, shampoo, hair dryers, hair styling products, high chairs, booster chairs, irons and ironing boards, journals, jungle gyms, latchkey kits (yarn), makeup for all complexion types (new cosmetics only), needlepoint kits, Nerf ® toys (balls, etc.), plastic tumblers, portable play tables, puzzles, blocks, skill-building mazes, construction materials, radios, robes and slippers, sand boxes and sandbox toys, school supplies (notebooks, pens, pencils), socks (women's and children's), pantyhose (all sizes), towels, wash cloths, umbrellas, vacuum cleaners and wagons.

They can also use backpacks, underwear (all sizes), furniture, pots and pans, pillows, bedding, business attire, socks, towels, day planners, wall calendars, night lights, laundry baskets and books for adolescents.

The shelters themselves can use laundry detergent, house plants, fish tanks, book shelves, computers, cordless phones, DeskJet and laser printers, desks (with or without locks), fax machines, flip charts, filing cabinets (with or without locks), safes, folding tables and chairs, living room chairs, modern telephone equipment, office supplies (general), photocopy and answering machines, speaker's lectern, overhead and slide projectors, VCRs, lamps, storage shelves, tables and chairs, video camcorder (for training), whiteboards or blackboards, and washable vinyl sofas.

Adoption Services

Many adoption agencies need "interim" items for babies and young children to help meet the needs of their small charges between hospital or foster care and going home to their new parents.

They can usually use disposable diapers, juice, cereal and formula (especially Similac®, Isomil® and Enfamil®), baby clothes, baby towels, diaper bags, receiving blankets, car seats, rocking chairs, changing tables, infant front-carry packs, bouncy seats, crib sheets and new plastic mattress covers, receiving blankets, crib blankets and strollers or baby carriages.

A contact that can help you find your local group is the National Adoption Center (215) 735-9988.

AIDS Hospices

Hospices provide physical, emotional and spiritual support for people and families dealing with this life-limiting disease. They need tape recorders and tapes, stereos with CD players, large TVs and VCRs, hymnals, bibles, blank writing journals, games, wall shelves, night lights, potted plants, bird houses and bird seed. They can also use popcorn machines, slushy machines, and soft-serve ice cream machines and baby monitors. Other appreciated items are room air filters and humidifiers.

AIDS networks would like grocery store gift certificates, cab passes, movie theater tickets, videos, pre-paid long-distance phone cards, and Britta® water-filtration pitchers and replacement filters.

The leading world-wide non-profit organization in conducting pediatric HIV/AIDS research and other serious and life-threatening diseases that affect children is the Elizabeth Glaser Pediatric AIDS Foundation. They need donated airline tickets and/or frequent flyer mileage, free warehouse space and/or freight services, donations of photocopiers, plain paper fax machines and Macintosh computer equipment.

Elizabeth Glaser Pediatric AIDS Foundation
2950 – 31ˢᵗ Street #125
Santa Monica, CA 90405
Phone: (310) 314-1459
FAX: (310) 314-1469
Email: info@pedaids.org

American Indian Ministries

Despite the apparent prosperity of many of the larger tribes that operate casinos, there are still many smaller tribes whose members are destitute and live in poverty. The sad fact is that there are some Indians who are so poor, that some Americans who are usually classified as poor look wealthy by comparison.

Widow's Mite Mission needs clothing, shoes, housewares, blankets, bedding, sewing fabrics and notions, seeds, tools, candles and candleholders (The Navajos they serve have no electricity), books, Christian cassettes and batteries, pots, pans, envelopes, stamps, toys, S&H Green Stamps, Gold Bond and Blue Chip stamps. They can also use medicines, vitamins and nutrients (even partial bottles) and food.

Widow's Mite Mission
P.O. Box 2
Cameron, AZ 86020

Shipping address for sending UPS shipments is:

Widow's Mite Mission
HC 33, Box 432
Flagstaff, AZ 86004-8801

Another Navajo ministry is the Four Corners Home for Children of the Navajo Reservation. This Home for homeless and helpless children provides temporary emergency care for children in dangerous situations. The also provide year-round live-in program for children whose parents suffer from alcohol, drug problems, divorce, etc.

Navajo Missions Four Corners Home
2103 W. Main Street
P.O. Box 1230
Farmington, NM 87401
(505) 325-0255

The Billy Mills Youth Center's program "Running Strong for American Indian Youth" is eager for all labels in the Campbell's Label for Education program. They exchange these labels for free educational and athletic equipment for kids on the Cheyenne River Sioux Indian Reservation.

The Billy Mills Youth Center
8815 Telegraph Road
Lorton, VA 22079

Animal Protection Shelters and Animal Care

These are the organizers that care for lost or abandoned animals, care for animals who have endured abuse and cruelty, run spay and neuter clinics, wildlife preserves, and public and private zoos.

Shelters or groups that house animals can use digital thermometers, antibacterial hand soap, dog and cat beds and animal bedding, cat trees, kitten feeding bottles, flea treatment, flea collars, "Have-a-

Heart" wild animal traps, heavy duty garbage bags, humidifiers and vaporizers, treats, portable heaters and heating pads, towels, blankets and puppy training pads.

They need donations of pet food (dry and canned), hamster, guinea pig and gerbil food, rabbit food, horse treats, halters and lead ropes, humane traps, new rawhide chews, new washable pet toys, clean used blankets and towels, paper towels, Kleenex®, Kitty Litter®, litter pans, liquid bleach, leashes and collars (nylon or metal slip collars, buckle or snap collars). They also love to get gift certificates for PetsMart and Petco. They also need pet vitamins and animal crates (cardboard or plastic pet carriers), and metal exercise pens. They can especially use large Vari kennels and chain link kennels.

Groups who deal with large animals can usually use wire fencing, fence posts, posthole diggers and tractors.

Some shelters and animal organizations also solicit art, antiques, vehicles, coins, stock and real estate. They sell these items in on-line auctions to finance their operations.

Christian Veterinary Mission is a division of World Concern and CRISTA. Veterinarians play an important role in alleviating hunger and hopelessness in the Developing World and these are the veterinarians who live abroad, working with the poorest of the poor to share Christ's love through veterinary medicine.

They need veterinary and basic science textbooks published within the last ten years (unless timeless material), veterinary journals (complete sets of 5 years or more, published within the last 20 years), multidose syringes, any supplies that are not used or expired (no EXPIRED medications).

They need Emasculatome, long-acting antibiotics, dewormers (injectable and oral), large size disposable syringes, large size needles (14-18 gauge), basic surgical instruments (new and used, clean and sterilized items), diagnostic equipment that is functional and in good working order.

CVM asks that all proposed donations be cleared first before shipping by calling or writing them at:

Christian Veterinary Mission
19303 Fremont Avenue N.
Seattle, WA 98133
(206) 546-7589
email: cvm@crista.org

CVM's Animal Loveline is a pet memorial program that allows grieving pet owners or their veterinarians to give a gift to CVM in memory of a beloved pet. The donor receives a tasteful sympathy card acknowledging the loss and thanks for the gift.

Gifts of Animal Loveline are used to support CVM's overseas work and domestic ministries in Asia, Africa, Eastern Europe and Latin America. Overseas, CVM veterinarians provide training for rural people who depend on livestock for their survival. In North America, CVM enables veterinarians to serve their own communities, encourages veterinary students, and works on Native American reservations.

Another group that can use animal supplies is Dogs for the Deaf. They need new rawhide chews, soft dog treats, Milk Bones®, clean blankets, grooming scissors, batteries (AAA), (AA), and (9 volt), film (35mm and 600 Polaroid ®), a digital camera and TV stands.

Dogs for the Deaf
10175 Wheeler Road
Central Point, OR 97502
Voice/TDD phone: (541) 826-9220

In addition to organizations that help traditional pets, there are others that specialize in non-pet creatures. One such is the Whale Museum in Friday Harbor, Washington (98250). They could use binoculars, range finders, depth sounders, radar equipment, handheld VHF radios, kayaks and related gear. They'd also like a CD/DVD burner and Family Tree software for Orca genealogy.

At Risk Youth Shelters

Crisis intervention for runaway and homeless teens is a major need everywhere these days. And most cities have groups who help young people struggling with drugs, rebellion, alcohol, suicide, and other life-threatening problems. Most offer Christian counseling, transitional residences, job training, and food and clothing services, particularly to those with chemical dependency problems.

Common needs the providers have are for internet-compatible computers with printers, PC educational and game software (and manuals), office supplies, office machines, office furniture, book shelves, comfortable couches and chairs, camcorders, videos, art supplies, sheet music, pencil sharpeners, pool tables, billiard balls, pool cues, basketballs, Nerf ® soccer balls, backboards and hoops, new or gently used large coffee pots, board games, sports equipment, portable CD and tape players, "boom boxes" and fishing gear.

The residents need underwear, socks, warm clothes, winter coats, mittens and gloves, blankets, watches, backpacks, bags with zippers, sneakers, and teddy bears. They also need basic toiletries (shampoo, brushes, combs, and toothpaste), (new) lip balm, stocking caps, backpacks and watches.

Teen Challenge runs the largest, oldest and most successful Christian drug abuse rehabilitation programs anywhere with over 150 operations worldwide. There is probably one near you.

> Teen Challenge International
> 3728 West Chestnut Expressway
> Springfield, MO 65802
> (417) 862-6969

Springboard Home for Youth in Crisis is a Christian-based temporary shelter for young people in need of housing and counseling.

> Springboard Home for Youth in Crisis
> 36644 Nufer
> Tucson, AZ 85705
> (602) 887-8773

Youth Encounter Homes is a ministry providing long-term residential treatment and care of displaced and unwanted teenage boys. It is state-licensed.

Youth Encounter Homes, Inc.
P.O. Box 713
Van Nuys, CA 91408
(818) 378-7500

Other parenting support and assistance groups that deal with troubled youth include Tough Love and Parents Without Partners.

Blind and Visually Impaired

Items the blind can use aren't usually readily available from the average home. But for those who do have them, the following items can be put to good use by any number of organizations for the blind: adaptive aids in good working order such as canes and magnifiers, Braille writers, Braille note-takers and Braille printers, large print books and bibles, and recorded materials for the blind (such as bible on cassettes). They also enjoy Talking Books on tape. For ideas of local groups who could use these materials, contact:

National Federation of the Blind
1800 Johnson Street
Baltimore, MD 21230
email: nfb@nfb.org

Other Blind Services

Bible Alliance provides bibles, (both printed and on cassette), to the visually impaired and to religious programs in prisons and various institutions and facilities. They can use bibles in 25 languages.

Bible Alliance, Inc.
Box 1549
Bradenton, FL 33506
(813) 748-3031

Christian Blind Mission ministers in over 90 countries providing medical and educational services for the prevention and cure of blindness. They also operate schools and orphanages.

Items they need include optical equipment, ophthalmoscopes, Slit lamps, sutures, general medical equipment, wheelchairs, crutches, wound dressings, sterilizing equipment, surgical implements, exercise equipment, ray lamps, ultrasound equipment, parallel bars, treadmill, hearing aids, ear syringes, audiometers and Ortiscopes.

Christian Blind Mission Internations,
P.O. Box 175
1506 E. Roosevelt Road
Wheaton, IL 60187

Library for the Blind operates a circulating library of tapes and Braille books for the blind.

Library for the Blind
c/o Ministries for the Blind
1445 Boonville Avenue
Springfield, MO 65802

Guide Dogs for the Blind

Yes, you can donate (certain) dogs and puppies as potential guide dogs IF (and that's a big if) they meet the following criteria:

Puppies

Puppies must be no younger than 7 weeks old. They must be Labrador Retrievers, Golden Retrievers or German Shepherds.

For consideration, the dogs must have the following proof:

1. A.K.C. (or C.K.C.) registration of both parents

2. O.F.A.* certification and results (hips and elbows) *Orthopedic Foundation for Animals

3. C.E.R.F. results (eye examination) Canine Eye Registration Foundation

4. Complete pedigree and health record

5. Previous litter results (if any)

Adult Dogs

Adult dogs must also be Labrador Retrievers, Golden Retrievers or German Shepherds. Both male and females are accepted. To be eligible for program evaluation, the dogs must be between 12 and 26 months old. The dogs must be healthy, friendly and accustomed to people. They must have knowledge of basic obedience and willing to accept responsibility.

In the case of adult dogs, papers and registration are not necessary. No dogs are to be shipped until pre-approved by the school.

For more information contact:

Leader Dogs for the Blind
P.O. Box 5000
Rochester, MI 48308-5000
(888) 777-5332

Local animal organizations could use such items as dog crates, slip collars, leashes, dog harnesses and dog combs and brushes.

Breast Cancer

Making Memories Breast Cancer Foundation has many requests for camcorders for those who want to leave behind recorded messages to children, grandchildren, husbands and family members. They also request Southwest Airline Frequent Flyer vouchers, and time-shares at fun places for final family get-togethers.

Making Memories Breast Cancer Foundation, Inc.
P.O. Box 92042
Portland, OR 97042-2042
(503) 252-3955

Camps

Camps are temporary homes away from home, and thus need virtually everything that would be found in a home: large and small appliances, kitchen ware, furniture, desks, dressers, musical instruments, books and bookcases, metal folding chairs and lawn furniture.

They can also use all kinds of sporting goods such as ping pong tables, tennis and badminton racquets and nets, balls, bats and backboards, boats of all kinds, life preservers, water slides, weight sets, tents, sleeping bags, backpacks, all kinds of camping gear, vehicles and lawnmowers.

Other things camps can use are golf carts, ladders, wheelbarrows, large passenger vans, computers, sports theme decorations, light tables, clean videos, and new tarps.

There are camps of every description in all 50 states, just look in the Yellow Pages of your phone book. There are camps for kids with AIDS, cancer and terminal illnesses, Day camps, religious camps, camps for the handicapped, music camps, scout camps, horse camps, training camps and revival campgrounds for adults.

Children's Group Homes

Little people have special needs. They need scaled-down furniture, baby cribs, car seats, small furniture, sweaters and warm clothes, disposable diapers, little socks, mittens, underwear, baby formula, baby wipes, baby food, fruit juices, LOTS of paper towels, Play-Doh®, Crayons®, coloring books, soft toys, little cars and dolls and large playground equipment such as slides and swing sets. The facilities can always use vaporizers and humidifiers, and depending on location, dehumidifiers, swamp coolers, air conditioners and/or heaters.

Older children need toys, jigsaw puzzles, board games, Lincoln Logs®, Legos®, baseball bats, balls and gloves, cards, modeling kits, glue, paint brushes, videos, beanbags and backpacks, rubber balls and hula hoops.

Groups that care for children are AIDS baby care hospices, group receiving homes and orphanages, foster parent organizations, homes for troubled youth, runaway shelters, and shelters for abused children.

St. Jude's Ranch is a home for abused, abandoned and neglected children. Under the direction of an Episcopal priest, its goal is in grounding the children in faith and teaching them to become responsible adults.

Much of their equipment is "paid for" by redeeming Campbell Soup labels and General Mills box tops. In one recent year, the proceeds from two million labels collected enabled the purchase of two new vans for the home.

St. Jude's Ranch for Children
100 St. Jude Street
Boulder City, Nevada 89005

Christmas Ministries

A simple shoe box filled with little toys, school supplies, hygiene items and trinkets, might go half way around the world to brighten the life of a child in a troubled country like Bosnia, Lebanon or Afghanistan. The box might also stay right here in the U.S. In short, the boxes go where they are needed.

Operation Christmas Child is a project of Samaritan's Purse, the Christian ministry led by Franklin Graham, son of Dr. Billy Graham.

The boxes can contain small toys such as little cars, dolls, stuffed animals, kazoos, harmonicas, yo-yo's, pens, pencils, crayons, stamps and ink pads, coloring books, writing pads, a toothbrush, soap, comb, a washcloth, hard candy, lollipops, mints, gum, sunglasses, flashlights (with extra batteries) socks, baseball caps, costume jewelry, hair ribbons and barrettes, watches and small picture books.

Upon receipt of the box Operation Christmas Child will also tuck in a brochure of Christian literature in the child's own language. During early November, the boxes can be dropped off at neighborhood churches all across America for shipment to North Carolina. Call the number below for a list of collection sites near you. You can also mail them year round to the following address:

Operation Christmas Child
c/o Samaritan's Purse
801 Bamboo Road
Boone, NC 28607
(800) 353-5949

A complete list of how to pack, mark and ship the box is on their website at www.samaritan.org/home.asp

Another program that also sends Christmas boxes to needy children is:

The Box Project
87 East Street, 2nd Floor
Plainville, CT 06062
(203) 747-8182

Toys For Tots (Marine Corps Annual Toy Drive)

These local toy collection campaigns begin in October and lasts until December 22. Toy distribution normally takes place on December 23 and 24th. Members of the community drop off new unwrapped toys in collection boxes positioned in local businesses. Marine Corps coordinators pick up these toys and store them in a central warehouse where the toys are sorted by age and gender interest.

At Christmas, coordinators, with the help of local social welfare agencies, church groups, and other local community organizations, distribute the toys to the needy children of the community.

To find the closest address where you can drop off new unwrapped toys, call your closest local Marine recruiter.

Child Protection (Prevention of Child Abuse)

Some of these groups provide in-home support, education, resources and advocacy to first-time parents, parents with cognitive limitations and help for limited-ability parents of preschoolers.

They need haircutting equipment (or certificates for haircuts), bus passes, non-violent educational videos, books, toys to age 8 and infant stimulation toys, baby books, new infant and children's clothing (to age 8) including socks and underwear, gently used maternity clothes, baby furniture, dressers, swings, highchairs, exercisers, strollers, dishes, silverware, kitchen and bathroom towels, pacifiers, thermometers, baby monitors, sippy cups and school supplies.

Clothing

Dress for Success needs dress suits and accessories for women re-entering the work force. Specifically what they want are coordinated contemporary interview-appropriate skirt and pantsuits. They also want beautiful blouses, blazers and jackets. They especially need larger size outfits. They also need professional type shoes, coats, umbrellas, raincoats, jewelry and scarves.

There are 70 groups around the U.S. and several more overseas. To contact a local group, check on their website at www.dressforsuccess.org

A Christian version of this same worthy aim is "Martha's Closet," a similar ministry run by various church denominations. To find a local group, start by checking with Episcopal and Anglican churches.

Got a pretty old bridesmaid dress or evening gown you no longer need? There's a group in Chicago that attempts to match every underprivileged "Cinderella" in Chicago schools with a beautiful dress and accessories to wear to her prom.

They need formal dresses, matching shoes or evening shoes, purses, jewelry, unopened cosmetics and hosiery. The organization sets up "boutiques" where the dresses and accessories are distributed. Volunteers serve as "personal shoppers" to the young women, helping guide each young woman through the boutique, helping her select dresses to try on, suggesting any necessary alterations, and coordinating accessories. Thus far, the Chicago group alone has helped 2,300 young women attend their proms in style.

There are similar prom dress programs in California, Florida, Georgia, Hawaii, Kentucky, Illinois, Louisiana, Maryland, Massachusetts, Minnesota, Missouri, North Carolina, Nebraska, New Jersey, Nevada, Ohio, Oklahoma, Oregon, Pennsylvania, South Carolina, Tennessee, Texas, Virginia, Washington, Wisconsin, West Virginia and Washington D.C. To find groups in these states email them at

info@glassslipperproject.org

Dress Donations for the Chicago group can be sent via UPS or FedEx ONLY (U.S. Mail not accepted) to:

The Glass Slipper Project
c/o Midway Moving & Storage
2727 W. Chicago
Chicago, IL 60622
(312) 409-4139

Warm winter clothes are needed by "Coats for Russia," This group collects used coats, blankets and sweaters for needy families in Russia and other Eastern Bloc countries. Voice of the Martyrs is an interdenominational missionary organization serving the persecuted church

Voice of the Martyrs
Coats for Russia
200 E. Frank Phillips Boulevard
Bartlesville, OK 74003
(800) 747-0085

Community Social Services

These organizations provide such valuable local services as teen health clinics, homeless outreaches for both men and women, emergency shelters, emergency feeding programs, food banks, clothing banks, senior centers, and such services as driving people to doctor appointments.

They need such things as toiletries, shampoo, soap, deodorant, feminine hygiene products, toothbrushes and toothpaste, food boxes (usually containing canned goods and items that don't need cooking), durable warm clothing such as jeans, sweatshirts and coats, blankets and sleeping bags.

Live-in shelters need beds, mattresses, bedding, couches and tables, chairs and lamps.

There are also organizations such as "Friends of Parks" and other neighborhood groups who maintain parks. They can use transplantable trees, shrubs, seeds, sandbox toys, sand, topsoil, wood chips, crushed rock or bark, lawn sod or seed, picnic tables, barbeques and climbing structures.

Crime Prevention

Prison Fellowship Ministries Angel Tree ® program represents the only national effort, religious or secular, to reach out to the children whose fathers and mothers are behind bars. For the past 18 years, Angel Tree® has reached thousands of children each year (more than 4 million since its inception) with Christmas gifts delivered on behalf of the prisoner-parent by church volunteers. These gifts bring hope and reconciliation to families separated by incarceration. This is a Chuck Colson ministry.

Angel Tree
P.O. Box1550
Merrifield, VA 22116-1550
Phone: (800) 55-ANGEL
FAX: (703) 456-4008
Website: www.angeltree.org

Deaf Services

This organization, which is a division of the Assemblies of God denomination, serves the deaf in the Philippines. They need hearing aids.

Bible Institute for the Deaf
1445 Boonville Avenue
Springfield, MO 65802

Developmentally Disabled

The mission of the ARC of the United States (formerly known as the Association for Retarded Citizens) is to represent the needs and interests of children and adults with mental retardation and their families. ARC has over 1,100 local chapters in the U.S. and is the largest voluntary organization of its type.

Frequently requested items they can use are: after-shave & cologne, artificial Christmas trees, arts and crafts supplies, basketballs, baskets, bathrobes, belts and suspenders, body sprays, bubble bath & bath oil, Christmas ornaments, comforters, compact discs, construction paper, costume jewelry, craft supplies, crayons and coloring materials, garland, glitter, greeting cards, hair accessories, hair conditioner, hats, gloves, glue, glue guns and glue sticks.

They are also happy to get' holiday decorations, holiday edibles, jewelry, lace, ribbon, light fragrance perfume, make-up kits, nail polish & remover, paints and paint brushes, pantyhose, paper, posters, puzzles (large piece), rain hats, scarves, silk plants/flowers, slippers, slipper socks, socks, straw hats, squiggle paints, Styrofoam shapes, sweatpants/ sweatshirts, (sizes M, L or XL) tights, tracing paper, umbrellas, videos (G/PG), wall hangings, wallpaper borders, watches, wrapping paper and wire.

Group homes can always use recliner chairs, framed pictures, sporting goods, puzzles and manual, board, card and computer games, video cameras, VCR's, TV carts,

These programs are always in need of items in good like-new condition that can be used as Christmas and birthday gifts. Check with your local school or institution, or contact The ARC of the US to find your local affiliate.

The ARC of the United States
500 E. Border St., Suite 300
Arlington, TX 76010
(800)-433-5255

Special Olympics

Special Olympics is an international organization dedicated to empowering individuals with mental retardation to become physically fit, productive and respected members of society through sports training and competition. Special Olympics offers those children and adults with year-round training and competition in 26 Olympic events.

They can use color laser printers, outdoor furniture, 10'x10' tents, VHS Camcorders, push lawn mowers, transportation, office equipment and supplies and sports equipment.

To get in contact with a local group, contact the national office at:

Special Olympics, Inc.
1325 G Street, NW, Suite 500
Washington, D.C. 20005
Phone: (202) 628-3630
FAX: (202) 824-0200

Special Education Schools and Programs

Skiforall is a year-round outdoor recreation program for students with physical, developmental and sensory disabilities. Volunteers donate conduct a program that features Nordic and Alpine skiing and participation in the Special Olympics.

Items they need are: an RV (Recreational Vehicle), a mobile shed, and a van. These items are needed to provide shelter, storage and transportation for program participants, volunteers and their equipment. They also need: a Kodak slide projector and projection screen, and an all-in-one TV and VCR for training and fund raising presentations. Also needed are skis, rain ponchos, cordless drills, heavy-duty staplers, copier paper, Pagemaker for Mac, a scanner and a vacuum cleaner.

> Skiforall
> 1621 114th Ave. SE, Suite 132
> Bellevue, WA 98004-6905
> (206) 462-0978

Disaster Relief

As explained earlier, please call first to determine exact needs before sending any item to a disaster site.

Many folks have the mistaken notion that Red Cross is the primary disaster relief organization, but that is not true. The following organizations all have long histories of providing disaster relief.

When there's a disaster, the Salvation Army is traditionally "the first on the scene, and the last to leave," honoring a century-long commitment to serve "those in need at the time of need and at the place of need." They provide whatever is needed:" mobile feeding, shelter, reconstruction, and financial assistance.

> Salvation Army
> P.O. Box 615
> Alexandria, VA 22313
> (703) 684-5500

Church World Service Disaster Response Office (CWS) coordinates the efforts of (many) Christian emergency services at home and abroad.

Church World Service Disaster Response Office
475 Riverside Drive #606
New York, NY 10115
(212) 870-3151

Adventist Community Services (ACS) takes disaster donations in advance of disasters, and has a computerized inventory of supplies ready to ship from their national clearinghouse when needed. They are REALLY well organized!

Adventist Community Service (ACS)
12501 Old Columbia Pike
Silver Spring, MD 20904-6603
(800) 381-7171 or (301) 680-6400

Lutheran Disaster Response (ELCA) helps by repairing and rebuilding homes, and doing such things as repairing roofs, and providing food, furniture and equipment following an emergency.

Lutheran Disaster Response
ELCA Domestic Disaster Response
8765 West Higgins Road
Chicago, IL 60631
(800) 638-3522 or (773) 380-2822

The Mennonites are workers too! They send in clean up and repair crews that pitch in with repairing and rebuilding. They provide sheetrock, carpentry, electrical and plumbing assistance.

Mennonite Disaster Service
1018 Main Street
Akron, PA 17501
(717) 859-2210

Northwest Medical Teams distributes humanitarian aid (medicines, supplies and food) to beneficiaries in more than 50 developing countries, locally in the Pacific Northwest, and to 40 other charitable organizations.

Northwest Medical Teams, International
Box 10
Portland, OR 97207-0010
(503) 624-1000

These groups can usually all use cleaning supplies, good mops, buckets, brooms, rakes, shovels and Shop Vacs®.

Drug and Alcohol Abuse

The twin demons of drug abuse and alcohol addiction are the root cause of the problems addressed by many, if not most of the organizations in this book. When either or both get a grip on a person, the resulting grief and troubles are like pebble ripples in a pond.

These are not victimless addictions. Their victims are the abusers themselves (who pay with sad wasted lives), innocent babies born as "crack babies", drug dependent or with Fetal Alcohol Syndrome, children who are battered, neglected and abused, and teens who live in insane worlds of no love, safety or security. Families, friends and employers join the list of those used and abused too, as does the community and society at large. We all pay the price.

That price includes innocent people killed by drunk drivers, mental impairment, dropouts or dismal academic performance, accidents leaving maimed and crippled victims, broken marriages, lost jobs, suicides, murders, venereal disease, and the dreams of a new generation shattered.

More than 50% of our 2,000,000 state and federal prison inmates are serving time for drug-related offenses, creating a $20 billion dollar problem for American taxpayers each year.

In addition to the many worthy groups on these pages that faithfully work to help those who have these problems, there are many other good groups not listed that could also use your help and donations.

There are the "proven-track record" groups like Teen Challenge, the Twelve-Step Programs, like Alcoholics Anonymous, Al-Anon and Alateen, Alcoholics

Victorious, Families and Friends of Alcoholics, Marijuana Anonymous, Narcotics Anonymous, Mothers Against Drunk Driving, One Step at a Time, Big Brothers and Big Sisters, and countless community anti-drug coalitions.

Every dollar spent on treatment saves more than $7 in crime, business losses and health care costs. We MUST win the war on chemical dependencies. Not only are our young people at risk, so is the future of our nation.

Emergency Services and Community Services (Local)

These include regular and volunteer Fire Departments, Police and Sheriff departments, Search and Rescue Units, Civil Air Patrol, Marine Patrols and Crisis Hotlines.

These good folks can use all sorts of things: Emergency radio equipment, cell phones, First Aid supplies, stretchers, tents, boats, boots, four-wheel drive vehicles, aircraft, mountaineering gear, avalanche beacons, climbing ropes, "sniffer dogs," snowshoes, computers, vans and motor homes which can be used as command centers, good local terrain maps, Global Positioning System receivers, sleeping bags and anything else which might be needed in a search and rescue or an emergency of any type. They like to carry a supply of Teddy Bears too.

Farm and Large Animal Groups

These groups include 4-H, Future Farmers of America, Future Homemakers of America, Granges and County Extension Agents. They all teach the old-fashioned values of hard work, responsibility, tackling long-term projects, clean living and training to be "salt-of-the-earth" adults.

A gift to these organizations is an investment in America's future and the future of our nation's food supply.

If you have any spare cattle or farm animals that need a good home, you can't hope for a better recipient than an FFA young person. They can use lots of animal feed too, as well as saddles, blankets, horse feed, all kinds of tack and supplies, fencing and tractors.

Windrush Farm Therapeutic Equitation, Inc. is a non-profit working horse farm that therapeutically challenges and rewards the disabled. They use horses to expand the personal, emotional and physical boundaries of all who ride with them.

Their wish list includes donations of sound gentle "therapy" horses (patient horses that can be ridden by crippled or emotionally-challenged children), round feed tubs, a heavy-duty leather hole punch, replacement stirrup elastics, double-ended snaps, screw eyes, hand saw, fly spray, horse blankets, shavings, gel pads, wormer, clipper blades, waterproof saddle covers, double elastic girths, and post and rail fencing.

Windrush Farm Therapeutic Equitation, Inc.
26 Brookview Road
Boxford, MA 01921
(978) 682-7855

Food Providers and Food Recovery Programs

In addition to foods, food banks also can use good working freezers, disposable diapers, jars of baby food, baby formula, baby wipes, personal care items (new toothbrushes and toothpaste), dishwashing and clothes detergents, paper towels, napkins and toilet paper and sanitary napkins.

Fresh foods are always welcome, as are canned meats (especially fish and chicken), canned goods (especially cranberry sauce), complete meals in a can (such as stew, meat-balls and spaghetti, chili with meat), boxed macaroni and cheese, evaporated milk, dry powdered milk, crackers, and seasonal treats. (Fruitcakes welcomed here). Food banks also love to get peanut butter and jelly, tuna fish and any commercially canned fruit.

Second Harvest is the nation's largest network of food banks. They operate 200 local food banks and collect and redistribute surplus food directly into the communities where it is needed. 23.3 million people turned to the agencies served by second Harvest in 2001, an increase of over 2 million since 1997. Forty percent were from working families.

Chicago-based Second Harvest handled more than 800 million pounds of donated goods in just one year. This represented more than $1 billion worth of donations. Other food banks around the nation have similar success stories in recovering and putting to good use millions of dollars worth of good food.

Gleaner's Groups are frequently tied in with local Second Harvest organizations. Farmers and gardeners donate excess or second grade fruits and vegetables just for the picking. In addition to food, gleaner's groups can use canning kettles, jars, rings and lids, and vacuum sealing units and bags.

Garden groups who grow food for food banks can use excess berry bushes, transplantable fruit trees, birdseed, potting soil, compost, fertilizer, food dehydrators, chipper/shredders, Rototillers®, Weed Whackers®, lawn mowers, rakes, shovels, trowels and garden tools.

They can also use such items of equipment and services that help them operate day to day. They can use warehouse equipment such as forklifts, pallet jacks, pallet racks, office equipment, trucks, furniture, office supplies, computers and software.

Operation Blessing (an affiliate of Christian Broadcasting Network), is one of the largest of the Christian food providers. Operation Blessing normally receives its donations in bulk from growers, food chains, manufacturing and production facilities, distributors and other industry organizations rather than individuals.

Examples of donations they solicit include perishable and non-perishable food products: disaster relief and medical supplies, pharmaceuticals, building materials and supplies, clothing and textiles, seeds and agricultural tools, books, journals, educational materials and school supplies, and basic hygiene items.

If you happen to have a barn, warehouse or silo full of food or other foodstuffs to dispose of, give them a call. They have their own fleet of trucks and can pick up your donation if you have a big enough quantity.

Operation Blessing
977 Centerville Turnpike
Virginia Beach, VA 23463
(800) 759-000

Historical Societies and Museums

Since storage of things is their primary job, most historical repositories can use things like file cabinets, display cases, shelving, sturdy boxes, heavy duty dollies (for hauling boxes and displays), digital cameras, 35-MM cameras, movie cameras, art supplies, and maybe even a CD "boom box" for background music.

Many can also use vintage clothing, costumes, hats, fabric, trims, sturdy ladders and Klieg lights.

Homelessness and Housing

Habitat for Humanity is a private nonprofit organization that helps low-income families build and buy a home of their own. Applicants must provide at least 500 hours of "sweat equity" in helping build their future home. In addition to building materials, they are always in need of donated or moderately priced land on which to build houses. Habitat relies on donations of labor and cash for construction-related expenses.

They can always use saw horses, Shop Vacs®, wheel barrows, power siding shears, drywall benches, extension ladders, storage containers and sheds, and all power tools.

They can also use lighting and plumbing fixtures and miscellaneous construction equipment. Groups who help out can also use work boots, work gloves, wool socks, long underwear, wool hats, and warm outerwear.

Emergency shelter and short-term shelter providers need lots of bedding supplies. They need single beds, pillows and pillowcases, twin bed blankets, sheets and mattress pads, dish soap and paper towels, towels and washcloths, paper and plastic cups, glasses, plates and napkins, disposable diapers (large and extra-large) and shower mats.

The Association of Gospel Rescue Missions (AGRM) is a national non-denominational shelter organization with 294 shelters in most major cities. Rescue missions provide emergency food and shelter, youth and family services, rehabilitation programs for the addicted, education and job training programs and assistance to the elderly poor and at-risk youth.

One in every three homeless men seeking refuge at a network of shelters is a veteran. They carry with them a variety of problems: post-traumatic stress, drug and alcohol abuse, depression and a variety of physical ailments. Their needs are food, warm coats and warm winter clothes, long underwear, sleeping bags and blankets, used suitcases, watch caps, ponchos, umbrellas, toothbrushes, toothpaste, water resistant clothing, socks, underwear, bandages, cough drops, dry dog food, padlocks, and flashlights and batteries. Needless to say, they always need help with housing, counseling, job training and rehabilitation.

To find an affiliate Mission in your area, call (800) 624-5156 or go to their website at agrm@agrm.org

Other noteworthy missions are:

The Bowery Mission
P. O. Box 455
Chappaqua, NY 10514

Light House Mission, Inc.
1200 Eagle Street
Terre Haute, IN 47807

Pacific Garden Mission
646 S. State Street
Chicago, IL 60605
(312) 922-1462

In addition to Missions, groups who provide short term and interim housing include the YWCA and YMCA, Salvation Army and American Red Cross.

Also at holiday time, remember that any group who houses people can always use Christmas decorations and gift items.

Hospital Assistance

Each Ronald McDonald House is a home-away-from-home for the families of children who come to nearby medical facilities for diagnosis and treatment of serious and long-term illnesses. Each of these wonderful facilities offers parents and their children emotional support, cheerful surroundings and inexpensive, safe residential accommodations while their children receive medical care.

Each Ronald McDonald House is self-supporting, and their needs include: aluminum foil, antibacterial hand soap, bleach, coffee (regular and decaf), colored copy paper, cooking oil, dishwashing soap, emergency earthquake kits, film (35mm), light bulbs, flashlights and batteries, food storage containers, garbage bags, heavy paper plates, lemon oil furniture polish, Polaroid film, postage stamps, paper towels, plastic cling wrap, Sony PlayStation ® (and games), sugar, videos (children's) and Zip-Lock® storage bags.

As mentioned previously, most Ronald McDonald Houses also usually collect pop can pull-tabs that help fund their operation.

A similar hospital "home-away-from-home" group is The Children's House at Johns Hopkins. They need disposable cameras, Polaroid® film, laminating sheets, file folders, file labels, Avery labels #5160, hand-held hair dryers, dryer sheets, and safety bed rails.

The Children's House at Johns Hopkins
1916 McElderry Street
Baltimore, MD 21205
(410) 614-2560

Inner City Youth Assistance Groups and Ministries

For over 35 years Teen Challenge has offered its' services free of charge to young people who need help, but are the least able to afford it.

The drug epidemic knows no boundaries, and Teen Challenge runs the largest, oldest and most successful Christian drug abuse program. They have 110 centers in the US and an additional 150 located in twenty-six foreign countries to aid young people seeking help. They have one of the best success rates around, with 86% of Teen Challenge graduates being drug-free even seven years after completing the program!

Their program is based on Christian principles and funded entirely through donations. They offer spiritual, academic and vocational training, equipping their young people to return to society as responsible and productive citizens.

Some donated supplies are used to sustain the participants, and others are put to use in vocational training. What isn't needed is sold to cover expenses. In some cities, Teen Challenge runs Thrift Stores.

Recent items they have been looking for are vending machines, air compressors, plumbing supplies, cleaning products, mirrors, lighting fixtures, machinery, vehicles of all types and building supplies. To find your nearest Teen Challenge contact:

Teen Challenge International USA Headquarters
3728 W. Chestnut Expressway
Springfield, MO 65803
(417) 862-6969

Others who reach out to young people involved in drug and alcohol abuse and gang activity are:

Victory Outreach
Box 2427
La Puente, CA 91746

Midwest Challenge
3049 Columbus Avenue So.
P.O. Box 7364
Minneapolis, MN 55407
(612) 825-6871

Jewish Services

Where the Christian community has hundreds of ministries that cover specific areas of need, the Jewish Community has one excellent umbrella organization that works in a multitude of areas.

The Association of Jewish Family and Children's Agencies is an international (U.S. and Canada) endeavor that has 145 local groups (each called Jewish Family Service). Most local agencies offer specific services for domestic violence, addiction and recovery, children's services (including adoption and foster care), senior needs (including eldercare and help for caregivers), food banks, emergency services (including emergency housing), and services to Jewish refugees and immigrants from the former Soviet Union and elsewhere.

They also deal with services for Developmentally Disabled adults and children (including group homes), and services to Holocaust survivors and their families. They also help folks with AIDS.

Each local Jewish Family Service is autonomous and each has different needs. Most can use food donations, and some can use furniture. They also solicit donated vehicles and stock. To find the closest Jewish Family Service group and what they can use, contact:

Association of Jewish Family
and Children's Agencies
557 Cranbury Road, Suite 2
East Brunswick, N.J. 08816-5419
(800) 634-7346
email: AJFCA@aifca.org

Libraries

Rural libraries need books, computers, audio visual equipment, manuals, tutoring aids, ESL (English As A Second Language) aids, GED aids, vans (for bookmobiles, teaching software appropriate for limited-English users, bookcases, tables, chairs, lamps, picnic tables, (occasionally) playground equipment, and educational videos, tapes and records. They might also welcome your "clipping files" and historical material. (Especially files that relate to the local area they serve.)

Literacy

Literacy programs enable students with learning disabilities and illiterate adults to become better parents, workers and citizens. There are 350 locally-based programs around the U.S. run by Literacy Volunteers of America.

Operation Blessing (mentioned on page 226) has a very worthwhile "Pencil Case Kits for Disadvantaged Youth" program.

They want a transparent pencil case filled with 1 pack of crayons (8 colors), 1 pack of color pencils (12 colors), 1 pack of #2 pencils (5 pencils), 1 pack of glue sticks (2 glue sticks), 1 pack of erasers, 1 pair of scissors (child friendly), and 1 pencil sharpener.

Place all the items into the pencil case. They ask that you do not include any additional items. They also ask that you include $4 to help cover the cost of shipping and handling. Send checks or money orders only. Do not place the envelope inside the pencil case. Mail the pencil cases to them at:

Operation Blessing Pencil Case Kit
CBS
977 Centerville Turnpike
Virginia Beach, VA 23463

The Barbara Bush Foundation for Family Literacy has funded 309 family literacy programs in 44 states since it was launched by Barbara Bush in 1989. Sites, participants and programs vary, so contact this national office to see what programs in your area might need.

The Barbara Bush Foundation for Family Literacy
1112 – 16th Street NW, Suite 340
Washington, DC 20036
(202) 955-6183

Medical Care Providers (Overseas)

YWAM (Youth With A Mission) operates two large Mercy Ships that travel worldwide providing ophthalmic surgery, cleft lip and palate surgery, dental assistance, and other surgical procedures.

They can use dental tools, equipment and supplies, medical products including general surgical supplies, ophthalmic surgical instruments, supplies and medications and optical equipment for use in their optical clinics. These clinics provide prescription eyeglasses, however do not send them glasses. Instead give eyeglasses to your nearest Lions Club, because it is they who clean and index the glasses, then give them to Mercy Ships.

In all cases it is very important to call the Health Care Services Department of Mercy Ships (903) 939-7000, to determine their current needs before sending anything. They will then tell you where to send any goods they can use.

Mercy Ships International
P.O. Box YWAM
San Pedro, CA 90733

Another organization that operates a ship is Operation Search. Through their ship "La Gracia" they provide clothes, food, and medical aid in the Caribbean.

Operation Search
40 Kemble Street
Lenox, MA 01240
(413) 637-2241

Military and Veteran's Groups

Since their beginning in 1958, Missions to Military, Inc., has been ministering to service men and women through strategically located Military Christian Centers. Their Centers resemble a "home-away-from-home" with free bunks, meals, recreation and Bible studies.

Missions to Military, Inc.
P.O. Box 6
Norfolk, VA 23501

Or

Missions to Military, Inc.
2221 Centerville Turnpike
Virginia Beach, VA 23464
(757) 479-2288

Other groups that might want to donations to aid active duty military personnel or veterans are: The American Legion, Disabled American Veterans (DAV), Old Soldier's Homes, Prisoner of War groups, Veterans of Foreign Wars and USO lounges at military bases and major airports. USO lounges need games, snacks, magazines and books.

Those in Veterans and Military hospitals might appreciate games, puzzles, writing paper, new greeting cards and note cards, stamps, and magazines of interest to men. American Red Cross and USO both collect these items. USO lounges also need fresh fruit, chips, pretzels, cups, local event tickets and playing cards.

A 1999 federal law requires the military to dispatch an honor guard to a veteran's funeral to fold the flag and escort the coffin when one is requested, but they aren't required to send a bugler. Instead they send a cassette tape of "Taps" to be played.

One group that believes our veterans deserve better than a taped "Taps" is Bugles Across America. Their buglers attempt to play a live rendition of "Taps" at the funeral of as many local veterans as they can.

With so many World War II veterans now in their eighties, more than 580,000 veterans are expected to pass away this year (at an average of 1,600 per day). That means this group needs a multitude of buglers to help pay their final tribute.

All horn players (and drummers) are welcome, from ex-military personnel, to just plain civilians (plus those from high school bands and symphonies). Bugles Across America also needs old military dress uniforms, horns, and drums.

Bugles Across America
Tom J. Day, Founder
1824 South Cuyler Avenue
Berwyn, IL 60402-2052
Email: tomjday@aol.com

Missing Children

Over 900 children are kidnapped by strangers or relatives every day. The Polly Klaas Foundation volunteers react immediately to abductions, resulting in many children being brought home safe.

Items they want are used vehicles of all kinds, real estate, mobile homes, trailers and RVs, running or not.

The Polly Klaas Foundation
701 Scott Court, Suite A.
Novato, CA 94945
(800) 380-5257

Another organization that assists parents and law enforcement in the search and recovery of missing children is

America's Missing Children
8 W. 19th Street
Jacksonville, FL 32206
(800) 992-0383.

Muscular Dystrophy

The Muscular Dystrophy Association welcomes donations of medical equipment including used wheelchairs in good condition, (powered wheel chairs, both adult and child-sized are especially needed), hospital beds, walkers, and communication devices for their local MDA loaner closets. Donated items are made available at no cost to individuals with neuromuscular disease.

Individuals with MDA/ALS could also use "seat-lifters" (those gadgets that help lift raise "sitters" into a standing position), deep lipped plates that won't allow food to escape when pushed around, customized eating tools for those with no wrist motion, grippers and extension "picker-uppers," long-handled shoe horns, drink aids with long sippers, grippers to help grasp pens, straws, toothbrushes and forks, Water-pics® for flossing, no rinse shampoo and soap, clothes with Velcro® closures, sturdy bed raise and shower bars and grips, and long-handled back scratchers.

MDA summer camps also need an available supply of First Aid and related medical items to deal with the inevitable bumps and scrapes common to campers. If you have something you think they might need, or would like to find out more about the needs in your area, call your local Muscular Dystrophy Association.

Multiple Sclerosis'

If you're in the Pacific Northwest, there's a wonderful one-man operation called The Donor Closet that collects and redistributes all manner of medical and mobility equipment. They help not only those with MS, but anyone who has been turned down by Medicare, Medicaid or an insurance company, or is having financial difficulty.

Items they collect and recycle are: bathtub riser chairs, bedpans and urinals, canes (including "quads"), cervical traction systems, crutches (some four-arm), commodes, computer stands for wheelchair users, diabetic equipment, deodorizer units, exercise equipment, exercycles, foam rubber bed pads, hand pickers and clothes assister rods, hospital beds (electric), hospital bed patient trapezes, Hoyer lifts, IV stands, orthopedic back/foot and leg braces, oxygen tank carriers on wheels, oxygen tank holders, range of motion units/electric tables, scooter lifts, sleep apnea units, stair stepper exerciser, toilet safety frames, toilet seat risers, vehicle hand controls, walkers (all types), wheel-in shower benches, wheel-in shower stall units, (car) wheelchair carrier with trailer hitches, wheelchair car top carriers, wheelchairs (electric and standard manual – all sizes), Depends® and Ensure®, and many other miscellaneous medical items not listed.

They ask only that the items donated be clean and unbroken with all parts and attachments, and any instruction or operator manuals be included.

To donate, contact:

Bill Brayer
The Donor Closet
23910 – 102nd Avenue West
Edmonds, WA 98020
(206) 546-6431

Local MS Societies can usually direct you to similar medical equipment recyclers in other areas of the country.

Performing Arts, Theater and Dance Organizations

Nearly every town has a Little Theater group, and there's hardly a school that doesn't put on productions of all kinds. Many churches also put on special presentations and can use theatrical supplies.

Such items include stackable chairs, folding chairs, chair dollies, bulletin boards, reader boards, garment bags, costumes, projection screens, wardrobe boxes, vacuum cleaners, electric saddle staplers, 6-8 foot tables, black light projectors, lighting equipment, and video cameras.

Prison Ministries

There are a number of good prison ministries, but many are either run by chaplains, or groups such as Full Gospel Businessmen, International. All are restricted as to what they can take in to prisons, and most are limited to bibles, Christian cassettes and Christian literature.

Prison Fellowship Ministries is the largest Prison outreach organization in the world. It was organized in 1982 with the idea that the cycle of crime could be broken by tending to the needs of those most likely to turn to crime and violence, —the children of prisoners. Prison Fellowship, founded by former Nixon aide Charles Colson, seeks to encourage and equip the church to help people suffering at all phases of the cycle of crime.

> Prison Fellowship Ministries
> P.O. Box 17500
> Washington, DC 20041-0500
> (703) 478-0100

If you have bibles you want to donate to a prison ministry, then give Prison Fellowship Ministries a call and they may be able to tell you of a bible bookstore in your area where you can drop off the bibles.

Other Ministries who may be able to use bibles for prisoners are:

> Good News Jail & Prison Ministry
> (719) 266-8652

> Institute for Prison Ministries
> (630) 752-5727

> Turning Point
> (800) 947-1993

Frequently prisons, jails and other assorted correctional institutions have academic programs and inmate libraries, and accept donated library materials for teenage to adult reading levels.

The State of Ohio, for instance, accepts fiction, non-fiction, reference books and textbooks less than 5 years old, illustrated series, books in Spanish, self-help books, books on parenting, and literacy materials for adult new learners. (Check with your own state to see if your penal institutions accept books.)

They do NOT want National Geographic magazines, romances or bound Readers Digest books.

Items may be shipped "Library Rate" to the attention of the librarian at the chosen institution, or donors may contact the librarian to arrange for pickup.

Refugee Resettlement Services

Most refugees who come to the US need everything. The various ministries who bring in refugees will find sponsoring families to house them the first few weeks, but after that, they'll have to set up housekeeping. Needed will be silverware, dishes, pots and pans, pillows, linens and towels, blankets, furniture, computers and TVs.

Newly arrived refugees and immigrants usually all need English dictionaries, and even more valuable to them are cross-reference English-native language dictionaries and language translation tapes, videos and software.

World Relief Corporation of the National Association of Evangelicals is one of the largest organizations at settling refugees into US communities. They have offices in most cities that are Ports of Entry into the US. In addition to household goods, they also need families to sponsor refugee families.

World Relief Corporation
450 Gunderson Drive
Carol Stream, IL 60189
(708) 665-0235

Rescue Missions

Frequently called "Soup Kitchens" these facilities traditionally serve the homeless with a warm meal, a place to get in out of the weather, and sometimes a bed at night. They serve as crisis intervention programs for the homeless, runaways, the drug and alcohol addicted and prostitutes.

Many operate under the banner of the non-denominational shelter organization International Union of Gospel Missions. One in every three homeless men seeking refuge at most of the shelters is a veteran. They carry with them a variety of problems such as post-traumatic stress, drug and alcohol abuse, depression and a variety of physical ailments.

Their needs are for food, warm coats and warm winter clothes, long underwear, sleeping bags and blankets, used suitcases, sewing supplies, world maps, globes (veterans like to point out their military travels), videos (PG, PG-13 or educational documentaries), bible study materials, notebooks and binders, arts and crafts materials, and indoor Christmas tree lights and decorations.

Many missions collect goods to give out to the clients. These items include towels, personal care items (toothpaste, toothbrushes, soap, shampoo, razors, deodorant), socks, underwear, pens, backpacks and duffle bags, men's winter clothing (large), bus tickets, telephone calling cards, peanut butter and jelly, stamps and envelopes.

Secular Groups

Other groups that might be willing recipients of in-kind gifts are Kiwanis, Lions, Rotary Clubs, Business and Professional Women, Alumni Associations, Boy and Girl Scouts, and Camp Fire Girls.

Senior Centers

Senior Centers truly are the centers of many "seasoned-citizens" lives. They operate programs ranging from hot lunches to day trips, adult day care, food banks, classes, dances, musical programs and resource banks of loaner equipment with items seniors need.

They can use a wide variety of gifts including busses, home heating fuel, fresh and canned food, medical supplies, fans, air conditioners, clothing, art and craft supplies, books and magazines, (especially large print), books on tape, dishes and utensils, food slicers, serving bowls and platters, large pots and pans, wheelchairs and walkers, large-screen TVs, large wall calendars, records, pianos, musical instruments, sewing supplies (yarn, knitting needles, thread, patterns), colored pencils, markers and coloring books, paper dolls and games (board games, Scrabble®, Monopoly®, playing cards, etc.). They can also use Bingo cages and balls, scrap-booking supplies, G-rated videos, sewing machines and quilting supplies, and ice cream makers.

Add to that warm flannel nighties and pj's, floor lamps, coffee air pots, greeting cards, dry eraser boards and pens, blood pressure cuffs, lava lamps, wheelchairs and wheelchair accessories, rubber balls.

Other things some seniors can use are mittens, gloves, scarves, warm new slippers, night lights and flash lights, filled bonus or freebie "frequent user" cards for barber and beauty shops, restaurants and foods, boxed holiday candy and small gifts for seniors (such as those bottles of perfume you'll never use).

Most can also use used (Pentium®) computers, printers, educational software, TV's, Satellite systems, gardening supplies, seeds, bulbs, pots, dirt, gloves and birdseed (and feeders), fish-tanks, exotic fish, sports equipment, and party treats and decorations, and bookshelves.

Senior Service providers include community senior centers, churches, older adult daycare centers, homebound care services and Alzheimer's caretakers.

Remember the Volunteer Chore Services too. These are the people who help seniors who can no longer care for themselves or their homes. These helpers can use Weed Whackers ®, lawn mowers, garden gloves, pruning shears, hedge clippers, flashlights, paint, saws and most power tools.

Unwed Mothers

These homes and services traditionally need maternity clothes, baby clothes, cribs, crib sheets and blankets, quilts, strollers, bouncy chairs, infant carriers, bottles, formula (especially Similac, Isomil and Enfamil), baby food, disposable diapers, humidifiers, bath towels and unopened in-date baby vitamins.

The Kansas City Youth for Christ operates two youth ranches and a crisis pregnancy center, a home with a capacity of 100 girls at a time, for pregnant teens.

Kansas City Youth for Christ
4715 Rainbow Boulevard
Shawnee Mission, KS 66205
(913) 262-1700

Loving and Caring
P.O. Box 146
Millersville, PA 17551

Another organization that cares for unwed mothers who have no place to turn is:

Metro Center for Family
Box 2590
Edmond, OK. 73083

They provide counseling for families and children, licensed child placement, and an adoption service for unwed mothers.

Youth Groups and Youth Service Providers

Groups who provide food, clothing and medical assistance to aid young people are:

Children International
2000 East Red Bridge Road
Kansas City, KS 64131
(816) 942-2000

Christian Appalachian Project
322 Crab Orchard Road
Lancaster, KY 40446-0001
(606) 792-3051

Compassion International
Box 7000
Colorado Springs, CO 80933
(800) 336-7676

In Canada, Compassion International's address is 99 Enterprise Drive S., London, Ontario N6A 5G8. They are a Christian child development organization that works with more than 100,000 children in thirty countries.

In Conclusion

Assuming the big job is finally done, and you have managed to find appropriate homes for a wide variety of your items, it was well worth the effort, wasn't it?

Those who have already done their disposing will tell you that they received far more from the experience than they gave. Also that in the process, they met many wonderful caring people, and many times felt like they were looked upon as angels, delivering exactly what was needed at the moment it was needed.

There's no explaining the "divine appointments" or "not-so-coincidental-coincidences" that soon become commonplace when you are the messenger who delivers needed goods at just the moment they are needed. Our only explanation is that God works in wondrous ways. Not only does God help those who help themselves, He also helps those who help others. You'll soon learn that in helping others, you will become a participant in miracles.

When this happens, and you have given the right item to the right person or group at just the right time, you will see for yourself that "little is much when God is in it!"

You'll also learn first-hand, that it truly is more blessed to give, than to receive.

May God richly bless you in this effort (and we know He will)!

Happy is the soul who finishes, having done well- +.

We would like to hear from you if this book helped to crystallize your thinking about how to dispose of your own stuff.

Also if you have any suggestions that may help others do their disposing, or if you know of other worthy recipient organizations, we would like to hear of those too.

Dunamis House
Box 321
Issaquah, WA 98027
bfilley@yahoo.com

Stuff Index

Recipient Index